The stories and strategies in this  hope and energy to anyone wa from loss.

When you have questions about the tough situations of life, you need a guidebook to get you through. This is that book—a must-read!

Karen Jensen knows about overcoming life's challenges. And she *really* knows how to encourage *you,* using true-life examples and God's Word. I highly recommend this book.

The crises of life come to us all. What is important is knowing what to do in the crisis. The answer is God's Word and knowing how to apply it in your case. Karen Jensen knows the Word and does the Word. Her easily understood wisdom can help you understand, as well as helping you to benefit others.

This book gives you permission to ask God all your tough questions—and then tells you how to get on with your life.

—Joe McGee

Author and Seminar Speaker

When your life is full of questions, Karen gives you lots of practical and biblical tools to help you get "unstuck." It's easy to read and full of faith. I really like this book!

—Patsy Cameneti

Author and Bible Teacher

Karen doesn't just talk the talk, but she also has walked the walk. She shares from her own journey—a journey that is full of inspiration and rich instruction. I invite you to learn from her experiences and insights. You'll be glad you did.

—Tony Cooke

Author and Bible Teacher

Karen has been a personal friend of mine for over twenty years. I watched her turn to God during the difficult time when her husband died, and I saw God truly turn her test into a testimony, her hurt into healing. Karen acted on God's Word all the way. I know you'll be tremendously blessed as you read this book, and I pray you too will be healed and encouraged.

—Kate McVeigh

Evangelist, Author, and Radio and TV Personality

WHY GOD WHY?

KAREN JENSEN

CHARISMA
HOUSE

Most CHARISMA HOUSE BOOK GROUP products are available at special quantity discounts for bulk purchase for sales promotions, premiums, fund-raising, and educational needs. For details, write Charisma House Book Group, 600 Rinehart Road, Lake Mary, Florida 32746, or telephone (407) 333-0600.

WHY, GOD, WHY? by Karen Jensen
Published by Charisma House
Charisma Media/Charisma House Book Group
600 Rinehart Road
Lake Mary, Florida 32746
www.charismahouse.com

Unless otherwise noted, all Scripture quotations are from the New King James Version of the Bible. Copyright © 1979, 1980, 1982 by Thomas Nelson, Inc., publishers. Used by permission.

Scripture quotations marked AMP are from the Amplified Bible. Old Testament copyright © 1965, 1987 by the Zondervan Corporation. The Amplified New Testament copyright © 1954, 1958, 1987 by the Lockman Foundation. Used by permission.

Scripture quotations marked ESV are from the Holy Bible, English Standard Version. Copyright © 2001 by Crossway Bibles, a division of Good News Publishers. Used by permission.

Scripture quotations marked GNT are from the Good News Translation in Today's English Version, second edition. Copyright © 1992 by American Bible Society. Used by Permission.

Scripture quotations marked KJV are from the King James Version of the Bible.

Scripture quotations marked NAS are from the New American Standard Bible, copyright © 1960, 1962, 1963, 1968, 1971, 1972, 1973, 1975, 1977, 1995 by The Lockman Foundation. Used by permission. (www.Lockman.org)

Scripture quotations marked NIV are from the Holy Bible, New International Version. Copyright © 1973, 1978, 1984, International Bible Society. Used by permission.

Cover design by Justin Evans
Design Director: Bill Johnson

Visit the author's website at www.karenjensen.org.

Library of Congress Cataloging-in-Publication Data:

Jensen, Karen, 1959-

Why, God, why? / Karen Jensen.

pages cm

Includes bibliographical references.

ISBN 978-1-62136-243-2 (trade paper) -- ISBN 978-1-62136-244-9 (e-book)

1. Consolation. 2. Change (Psychology)--Religious aspects--Christianity. 3. Loss (Psychology)--Religious aspects--Christianity. I. Title.

BV4905.3.J46 2013

248.8'6--dc23

2013011761

13 14 15 16 17 — 9 8 7 6 5 4 3 2

Printed in the United States of America

In loving memory to **Brent Jensen**, a larger-than-life kind of guy, who was full of fun, full of the Word, and walked in love better than anyone I've known.

To our sons, **Josh** and **Ryan Jensen**, who grew up half their lives without a dad but have matured into powerful, obedient, thoughtful, selfless, and fun-loving men of God. A mom couldn't be prouder. You guys are the best!

And to my wonderful daughters-in-love, **Jacqueline** and **Tara**, who have come along and made our lives exponentially *better* in every way.

Contents

Acknowledgments

ALMOST THE BEST part of writing a book is getting to acknowledge the people who have helped me get where I am today. When you read my story, you have to know there have been lots of people behind the scenes, walking alongside (even more than I've mentioned here), and I thank God for every one!

I have to start with Brett and Michelle Dunstan, because anyone who was around after my husband died knows that they were my Aaron and Hur. We wouldn't have survived without them. Thank you for laying down your lives. It'll take eternity to tell you. And right there with them were Clark and Sonni Hyvonen, Gary and Jeanne Armstrong, and Jackson and Deborah Taylor. They'll all tell you, it was the hardest time yet the *best* time of our lives because of God's faithfulness. Also Kelly Owen Welty, who made such beautiful music (still does) and who personifies grace under pressure...Joe McGee, who saw through us...Kevin and Nancy Johnson, who have always and faithfully been there...All these and our wonderful BFC family, I love you guys!

Pastor Kenneth W. and Mrs. Lynette Hagin, my pastors, who watched over us and helped in countless ways then, and whom I now get to work alongside in ministry, thank you. Thank you to my friends and fellow ministers of RMAI, region number one (the *great* Northwest Region)—my longtime besties Rod and

Rebecca Sundholm; Rick and Linda Sharkey; Gary and Kimberly Isbell; and Pastor Jann Butler. You came and preached and gave endless support. A special thank you to my dear friends Pastor Glen and Theresa Johnson, who never tired of helping my sons, my staff, and me in every way! And last, but by no means least, Tony and Lisa Cooke, who always checked up on us, praying for us and being there whenever we needed them.

And where would I be without my family: my wonderful parents, Dick and Ruby Lane; my uncle Rich Osburn, who taught me so many things about ministry and graciousness under fire; my Aunt Danna Osburn (aka St. Mom), who introduced me to Jesus and has simply prayed me through everything; Darren and Shelley Osburn; and Melinda Osburn Koehler, my heart-friend-turned-cousin, who is the closest thing I have to a sister on this earth—much love!

Fast-forwarding to today, I have to acknowledge Joyce Monk and Kelly Kissinger, my faithful daily e-mail friends—you mean so much to me. My "office family": Doug Jones, Joe Duininck, Ann Graves, Laura McKown, and Ryann Weaver, who make going to work a joy and who constantly encourage me. Not many people get to work every day with people of this caliber. And Tad Gregurich, who, it must be mentioned, patiently taught me the ropes the first few years and never closed the door between our offices. I'm forever grateful.

Fred and Lucy Kurz, *none* of this would be happening without you. You amaze me! Ephesians 3:20 is about you in my life. God sent you! Thanks for obeying Him! Wow, I'm so glad to be on this journey with you. J. P. Jones, master of websites and all things media; Mike

Taylor, whiz of video; and Dagny Griffin and all my tribe of writer friends—huge thanks for helping, encouraging and making me look so good!

Many thanks to Tessie DeVore, Debbie Marrie, Woodley Auguste, Jevon Bolden, and the great staff at Charisma House who took a chance on me and worked so hard to make this book happen—blessings and multiplied blessings to you!

Chapter One

IS IT OK TO
QUESTION GOD?

M Y HUSBAND, BRENT, went to bed early. It was New Year's Day 1997, and the preceding twenty-four hours had been crazy—real crazy.

As we did every year, we had rung in the New Year with our close-knit church family in Boise, Idaho. We had celebrated with games, prayer, and lots of good food. A few stragglers had hung around until about 2:00 a.m. As the pastors of the church we had been the last to leave, finally locking the doors and dragging ourselves home in the wee hours of the morning.

An emergency phone call from a church member awakened us very early on New Year's Day. Running on three hours sleep, Brent had climbed out of bed and gone to help them.

That day I had managed to sneak a nap in, but Brent hadn't. He and our sons, ages twelve and thirteen at the time, had watched every college football bowl game on television and even gone to a nearby park and played their own game with some neighborhood kids.

By 9:30 p.m. Brent could barely keep his eyes open. With a smile he leaned over and gave me a kiss.

1

"I love you," he said over the noise of the TV show I was watching.

"I love you too," I said, glancing up from my cross-stitch project and smiling at him as he walked toward the hallway.

When I went to bed, about an hour later, I found that Brent had stopped breathing. I called 911, and paramedics rushed to our house. They were unable to revive him, and later at the hospital he was pronounced dead.

"I love you" were the last three words we would ever say to each other on this earth. I'm sure thankful. It left me with no regrets.

Yeah, I Had Questions

As you can imagine, my life changed drastically after that night. Most significantly I became senior pastor of our church, and I became a single mom with the responsibility of raising our sons through their teen years—two things I had *never* expected to do.

When a heart-wrenching event happens, some people balk at asking God big questions, either fearing the answer or unsure that they should even ask. But not me. After that night, *I had questions.*

Man oh man, did I have questions!

Why, God, why? How did my big, strong, healthy thirty-seven-year-old husband, who hadn't been sick at all, simply go to bed one night and suddenly end up in heaven?

Why didn't You tell me? I was right in the next room watching television, for crying out loud! Why didn't You notify me so I could help him?

How could You let this happen? What about divine

health? What about Your protection? What about satisfying us with long life?

~~~~~~

I had questions...."Why, God, why?"

~~~~~~

Do You Have Questions?

This is my story. What about you? Sometimes life can be hard and painful. I wish there was a way to avoid the painful things altogether, but unfortunately there isn't. We live on an earth with the curse of sin, which means that awful things do happen. What has come about in your life that's caused you to ask, "Why, God, why?"

What occurrence has blindsided you? What painful event has stunned or dismayed you? Maybe your very foundation has been shaken by death, illness, a broken relationship, financial disaster, a bitter disappointment, or another life-altering circumstance. As a result you may be having trouble moving past the pain. You may be seriously doubting your faith in God.

First, please know that there is One who understands. God has a way to bring you through your hardest times.

Second, I'm glad you've picked up this book. I believe it can help you. Our heavenly Father is faithful, and He loves you so much. He doesn't want you stuck in the land of hurt. He has made a way out. He wants to heal your broken heart and help you embrace your bright future.

You Can Ask Why

At the beginning of the movie *Sleepless in Seattle*, Sam Baldwin (played by Tom Hanks) and his young son,

Jonah, are shown at the gravesite where Sam's recently deceased wife (Jonah's mother) is buried.

Sam tells Jonah, "Mommy got sick. And it happened just like that. There was nothing anybody could do. It isn't fair. There's no reason. But if we start asking why, we'll go crazy."[1]

I'm different than Sam Baldwin. I have questions, and I think they should be asked. My husband died suddenly in his bed at age thirty-seven without warning. I think there's room for questions in an event like that. I'm sure you have some questions too.

Maybe people have told you, "Don't question God." But I think that's ridiculous. Let's face it—you are asking questions anyway. In your heart and in your head you've probably already asked, "Why, God, why?" He knows what you're thinking, even when you keep silent (Luke 5:22; 24:38). So why try to hide your questions from Him? He can handle whatever you say. You cannot ask anything He has not been asked before.

Maybe people have told
you, "Don't question God."

Remember, God is your Father. He loves you! He already knows everything that has happened in your life, and best of all He also knows everything that *will* happen in your future—so who better to talk to when something hard happens?

We should ask God all the questions we want. In fact,

I think He is the *first* one we should ask. So go ahead, start asking.

Here are some honest questions you may have for God:

- Why did this happen?
- Why didn't You help me?
- Why did *You let* this happen?
- Why *hasn't* this been fixed or healed?
- Why can't I _____? (fill in the blank)
- Why is my life like this?
- Why is it taking so long?
- Did I miss Your will?
- Can I ever trust myself/anyone/You again?

You might have questions about something you have read in the Bible or something you have heard in a sermon. Maybe you have questions about bad things that have happened to other people or someone who received a miracle when you did not. Go ahead and ask the questions.

Be honest. Ask every scary, ugly, angry question that has already passed through your mind. You might even want to write your questions down and date them, maybe in a private journal or on a calendar.

Now What?

What you do with your questions once you have asked them is crucial. Sometimes an answer comes quickly. Other times it takes time (even a lot of time). And you might not like some of the answers you get! Then there are the questions that are never answered in this lifetime. You simply have to trust God.

Then once you've asked your questions, you need to *put them on the back burner.*

Let me explain with a simple illustration. When using a four-burner stove, you will do most of your cooking on the two front burners—that's where you prepare food that needs attention or requires action, the food you're thinking about most.

Once you've asked your questions, you then need to *put them on the back burner.*

The two back burners are where you put food that needs to simmer for a while. You are not going to give those dishes your full attention, or really even think about them much until they are done.

For example, if you are making homemade stew, first you put a pot on a front burner, where you brown the meat or add chopped veggies and spices. After all the ingredients are in the pot, you move it to a *back burner* where the food can simmer. You set the timer and forget about the stew, except maybe to stir it once in a while.

That's what you need to do with your questions. Picture yourself putting them into a big pot and then pushing the pot to a back burner.

You might pray something like this: *Father, here are my questions. Now that I've asked them, I'm going to put them on a back burner of my life and keep "cooking" on the front burners. I'm going to keep thinking about moving forward and growing in You. I'm going to keep reading Your Word, believing You, loving You, seeking Your will, and obeying what You tell me to do. I'm going to keep on trusting You.*

When you pray this kind of prayer, instead of camping out at your point of hurt, you keep your heart and mind on God's truth and His good plan for your life. Don't let your questions stand between you and God. Don't get mad and blame *Him* for the pain. He is your *help* in difficult times!

Don't be offended. Remember, God is your heavenly Father; He's on your side. Simply put, He is good, and Satan is bad. It wasn't God who caused terrible things to happen to you. The devil is the god of this world (2 Cor. 4:4), and that's why bad things happen (more on this in chapter 5). Right now just keep in mind that when you push your "questions pot" to a back burner, God is there to help.

Know God

Bad things happen to believers and unbelievers alike. When tragedy strikes, both will have questions. But the resolve will be different depending upon your relationship with God. It's impossible to trust God if you've never asked Him to be the Lord of your life. By that I mean you need to ask Jesus to be your Savior. That's how you become a member of His family and receive all of His blessings. That's how you get to heaven—there's no other way. Jesus said, "I am the way, the truth, and

the life. No one comes to the Father except through me"
(John 14:6).

Don't let your questions stand
between you and God.

If you haven't done so, now is the time to put your
old life behind and embrace a new one in Christ. When
you're a child of God, you're in position to ask Him all
the questions you want and receive His comfort and
help. If you haven't already asked Him to be your Savior,
you can do it now. Go to the back of this book and pray
the prayer of salvation you'll find there. Then come on
back and keep reading.

Keep Going Through!

One of my favorite verses is Psalm 23:4: "Yea, though I
walk through the valley of the shadow of death, I will
fear no evil; for You are with me; Your rod and Your
staff, they comfort me."

This verse lets me know that first of all, there is a valley
of the shadow. Stuff is going to happen in this life—it
just is. I wish I could wrap you in cotton and insulate
you so that bad things won't happen to you, but I can't.
Besides, that would be no kind of life. A real life has
challenges and risks. Without those, existence would be
dull indeed.

The key word in Psalm 23:4 is "through." Keep
walking *through* the valley of the shadow; don't set up
camp there!

The valley of the shadow is *not* a place you want to stay. Keep going until you come out the other side. And you can make it.

We've all met people who've allowed circumstances or a traumatic event to stop them in their tracks or even define their lives. Perhaps a loved one or best friend died, and they couldn't get past it. Maybe someone did them wrong, even a long time ago, and they're still rehashing it, blaming all their troubles on that horrible thing that happened.

Maybe you're the one who is stuck.

When something traumatic happens, it can sometimes make you feel as if you don't know anything anymore. You thought you knew what to expect. You thought you could count on certain things to always be there for you, or to always be the same—things such as God, a loved one, a friend, a business partner, the government, or the church. When something bad happens, you're not sure at all.

I thought I was going to be married to Brent my whole adult life. In an instant everything changed. I thought I would always be a wife, but after he died, I had no idea what my future looked like. The things I thought were sure had been irrevocably changed. Nothing seemed sure anymore.

I had questions!

Pain can seem to encompass every aspect of life, shaking you to the very core. You might feel like you can't possibly move on when you don't know what to expect in the future. You ask questions. *What if this happens again? How can I be sure of anything?* Sometimes it's terrifying.

I'm here to assure you that even though you may have questions, you haven't lost all perspective, knowledge, and wisdom. You *do* know some things. You might feel as if you're standing on shaky ground and that everything you once believed in is up for grabs, but there are still things that are very sure. Those are the things we're going to look at in detail.

> Keep walking *through* the
> valley of the shadow; don't
> set up camp there!

The main purpose of this book is to help you find out what to do *now*—now that you've asked your questions. What should you "keep cooking" on the front burners of your life? How can you keep living, loving, and serving while your questions simmer away on a back burner?

In order to break down camps of pain, sadness, regret, confusion, or disappointment, you have to ask questions, then put them on the back burners and trust God. Fear no evil because He is with you.

Trust God

During the weeks immediately after Brent died, I wasn't ready yet to start preaching three times a week, so ministry friends came to preach in our church. Inevitably at the end of most services the visiting minister prayed for me. I appreciated and needed the intercession. After each one prayed, I basked in the presence of the Lord— sometimes for up to an hour.

As I basked in God's presence, He ministered His wonderful comfort to my heart and spoke gentle reassuring words to my spirit. It was a sweet time of peace, and I felt like I could ask Him anything.

Often, after basking for a while, I would say, "Father, as long as we're here in this lovely quiet place together, is there anything You want to tell me about *what in the world happened?*"

Each time I asked, He patiently gave me the same answer: "Will you trust Me?"

I might not be the sharpest knife in the drawer, but I quickly deduced that it wasn't a good time to stop trusting God. Some people might back away or even get mad at God, but right then I needed Him more than ever. Running *away* from Him didn't seem as smart as running *toward* Him.

Each time He asked if I trusted Him, I said, "Yes, Lord." After about the eighth time we had this conversation, I finally promised, *I'll stop asking that, Lord. I still have questions, but yes, I will trust You.*

Proverbs 3:5 always reassures me: "Trust in the LORD with all your heart, and lean not on your own understanding." Every day I learned more of what it means to trust Him with *all* my heart, even if I didn't understand certain things. I knew that without Him I'd never be able to pastor a church, raise teenage boys, or get over losing my husband, so I chose to trust.

Don't Look Back

If you study the lives of successful people—in the Bible, in ministry, in sports, in Hollywood, or in the business

world—you'll find that many of them have had bad
things happen to them, and they all had questions.

One huge key to success in life is
the ability to leave things behind.

Despite their traumas or disappointments, they left
the past behind them, survived the pain, and moved on.
When they were knocked down, they got up. They per-
severed through heartache until they came out the other
side, stronger.

Some people who've had something bad happen to
them stop right there. The bad thing defines them, and
they never move ahead. My heart hurts for these people.

I truly believe that one huge key to success in life is
the ability to leave things behind.

The storms of life come to everyone. Despite how you
feel when down, you're not the only one who's had hard
things happen to them. *Everyone* has. It's what you *do*
in the midst of the storm that determines what happens next.

I remember watching a football game on television
where Jake Plummer was quarterback for one of the
teams. In that particular game Jake threw two or three
interceptions in the first three quarters. Then in the
fourth quarter he threw a game-winning touchdown pass.

Hank Stram was the television commentator that day.
After that touchdown pass he said, "Jake has what all the
great quarterbacks have—the ability to forget."

Isn't that the truth? Certainly Jake felt horrible each

time he threw an interception. But his failure didn't stop him from going back onto the field to throw more passes. He kept coming back, even after he was intercepted more than once. If he hadn't, he never would have thrown the game-winning touchdown pass.

I will never forget Hank Stram's comment. Jake Plummer managed to leave the past behind. It was the only way he could succeed and lead his team to victory. That's something we all want to learn how to do.

When I think of leaving the past behind, I also think of the apostle Paul, who wrote a large portion of the New Testament.

Here was a guy who early in his life had facilitated the beating and killing of Christians! But Jesus got hold of Paul (Acts 9), and he *became* a Christian. When he made his first attempts to preach Christ, all of the Christians feared him. But he kept on.

If anyone had a right to feel bad about his past and quit, it was Paul. Without God's help he could have been eaten alive by guilt. Or at the very least he could have chosen to stay in the background and never preached the Word. In Philippians 3 he provides some insight into how he overcame his past and kept moving forward with the Lord:

> Brethren, I do not count myself to have apprehended, but one thing *I do*, forgetting those things which are behind and reaching forward to those things which are ahead, I press toward the goal for the prize of the upward call of God in Christ Jesus.
> —PHILIPPIANS 3:13–14,
> EMPHASIS ADDED

Paul said he did *one thing* that helped him press forward in life: he forgot what was behind. I, for one, am glad he did—otherwise we wouldn't have a substantial part of the New Testament!

Peter also understood this principle about leaving the past behind. In Matthew 26 we see him vow his undying loyalty to Jesus (vv. 33–35). But then, almost right away, *three times* Peter denies he even knows Jesus (vv. 69–75). Wow. Now that's grounds for feeling guilty!

> You can ask your questions, put them on a back burner, and then continue "cooking" with God on the front burners of life, moving forward with Him.

But Peter didn't let that embarrassing moment define him. Even after Jesus was crucified, Peter chose not to camp out in the land of sorrow and guilt—instead he rose up and went to the Upper Room with the disciples on the Day of Pentecost. (See Acts 2.) After being filled with the Holy Spirit that day, he preached the sermon that won three thousand people to the Lord! (See Acts 2:14–41.)

Make that your goal—to forget what's behind and press forward. If Jake, Paul, and Peter did it, you can do it. You can ask your questions, put them on a back burner, and then continue "cooking" with God on the front burners of life, moving forward with Him. It's what I learned to do after my husband died, and it's what you can do too.

Think About What You're Thinking About

It's important to remember that *you* are the only one who gets to decide what you think about. You are the CEO of your thoughts!

You may feel like a victim—like things have happened *to* you that you have no control over. But no matter what happens, you always have control over your own thoughts. Nobody else is doing your thinking for you. You decide what to think about.

Take a moment to think about what you've been thinking about. Have you focused on your questions, letting them run over and over in your mind without restraint? Have you nurtured your thoughts of sadness, anger, fear, hurt, resentment, or disappointment, spending most of your time thinking on your pain and the circumstances surrounding it?

If so, those thoughts aren't taking you where you really want to go—into a bright future. In fact, they're probably making you miserable.

God's Word can help. Look at Philippians 4:8: "Summing it all up, friends, I'd say you'll do best by filling your minds and meditating on things true, noble, reputable, authentic, compelling, gracious—the best, not the worst; the beautiful, not the ugly; things to praise, not things to curse" (THE MESSAGE).

You are the one who chooses what will fill your mind. And if God tells us in His Word to do so, we can do it. You'll do best by filling your mind with good things!

Second Corinthians 10:5 tells us to take control of our thoughts: "Casting down arguments and every high thing that exalts itself against the knowledge of God, bringing every thought into captivity to the obedience of Christ." It matters what you think about!

As motivational speaker Earl Nightingale once said, "The mind moves in the direction of our currently dominant thoughts."[2] If your most dominant thoughts get stuck on things that have gone wrong, hurts that have been inflicted, or fears over trauma that has happened, you're going to get stuck there. If you don't lead your thoughts, your thoughts will lead you.

<hr>

You are the CEO of your thoughts!

<hr>

In order to move forward in your life and break out of the land of hurt and disappointment, you must first of all think about what you're thinking about. Then you must take control of any wrong thinking.

Replace Wrong Thoughts

How do you take your thoughts captive? You could try closing your eyes tight, balling up your fists and saying, "I won't think about this. I won't think about this. I won't think about this!"

Have you ever tried that? I have! If you're like me, in fifteen seconds or less you're back to thinking about the problem. Instead of willing yourself to stop thinking wrong thoughts, you have to *replace* them. You have to put something *else* in your mind. Of course, the best thing to put in there is God's Word. It's truth, and truth is what makes you free (John 17:17; John 8:32).

I like to call this process "thought replacement

therapy." It works like this: picture a glass full of orange juice. It represents wrong thoughts, so you want to empty the glass.

For the sake of this exercise let's say you have to leave the glass sitting on a flat surface—you can't tip it or turn it upside down. That's similar to the way your brain works. After all, you can't just tip yourself upside down to empty your head of wrong thoughts, can you? So how can you get the juice out of the glass?

Let's say that you also have a big bucket full of pure, clear, spring water. This represents right thoughts, in line with the Word of God.

If you start pouring that water into the glass full of orange juice (and keep pouring and pouring and pouring), what would eventually happen? Soon enough you'd have a glass full of nothing but beautiful crystal-clear water. All signs of the orange juice would be gone.

It's the same with hurtful thoughts. The best way to change them is to *replace* them with good thoughts. And the Word of God is the perfect replacement. Pour the cleansing water of the Word into your mind by thinking on what God has said. Go ahead, meditate on it. This will fill your mind with beautiful crystal-clear thoughts of peace, love, grace, and victory.

Simply put, in order to get *wrong thoughts out* you need to put *right thoughts in*.

Every time your mind wants to wander back to your questions or back to the land of bad thoughts (and it will!), you can *choose* instead to think on what God has said (things that this book is full of!).

Remember, you and only you are in charge of what you think about. When wrong thoughts come, you can say, "No, I take those thoughts captive. I'll remember what God's promises say."

If you don't lead your thoughts,
your thoughts will lead you.

This is one reason that it's good to memorize Scripture. Or at the very least keep Bible verses handy (on a card, your cell phone, or a sticky note stuck to your computer monitor) so you have immediate access to it when you need it.

It's very much like a bank account. You can't withdraw money from your account unless you've first made a deposit. You have to put God's Word *in* (read it, listen to it, spend time with it) so that it's in your mind when you need to make a withdrawal.

If you spend all your time thinking about your questions and the bad thing that has happened, you're going to get stuck. The only way to leave the pain behind and move forward is to change what you're thinking on.

Choose Positive Thoughts

There is a story I like about a ninety-two-year-old gentleman whose wife had just passed away.[3] They had been married for seventy years. He was legally blind and no longer had her around to watch after him, so he had to move to a nursing home.

On the morning of his move he was up by 8:00 a.m. and dressed in his best outfit. His hair was fashionably combed, and his face was perfectly shaved. In the car on the way to nursing home he hummed a happy tune. After he arrived, he patiently waited in the lobby as it took hours for the check-in process to be completed. Finally his room was ready. When told he could now go to his new quarters, he smiled sweetly.

As the old gentleman maneuvered his walker to the elevator, the attendant described the tiny room, including the eyelet sheets that had been hung on his window.

"I love it!" he stated with the enthusiasm of an eight-year-old who'd just been given a new puppy.

"But Mr. Jones, you haven't even seen the room yet," the attendant said. "Just wait."

"Oh, that doesn't have anything to do with it," Mr. Jones replied as they got on the elevator. "Happiness is something you decide on ahead of time. Whether I like my room or not doesn't depend on how big it is or how the furniture is arranged; it depends on how I arrange my mind. I've already decided to love it."

Mr. Jones went on to say, "It's a decision I make every morning when I wake up. I have a choice. I can spend the day in bed thinking about my aches and pains or how much I miss my wife, or I can get out of bed and be thankful that I'm alive and for the body parts that still work fine. Each day is a gift, and as long as my eyes open, I'll focus on the new day and all the happy memories I've stored away just for this time in my life."

Wow. I can't imagine what it would be like to lose a spouse after seventy years of happy marriage. And then on top of losing his wife, he lost his independence and had to move to a nursing home. There's plenty in this scenario to be sad or depressed about! It would be easy to cry out, "Why, God, why?"

⚬⚬⚬⚬⚬⚬⚬⚬⚬⚬⚬⚬⚬⚬⚬⚬⚬⚬⚬⚬⚬⚬⚬⚬

In order to get *wrong thoughts out*
you need to put *right thoughts in.*

⚬⚬⚬⚬⚬⚬⚬⚬⚬⚬⚬⚬⚬⚬⚬⚬⚬⚬⚬⚬⚬⚬⚬⚬

Yet Mr. Jones decided to be something other than sad or depressed. I don't know about you, but I think I'll choose to "arrange things in my mind" the way he did. I will choose to meditate on God's Word and be grateful for the good things I have.

Move Onto the Front Burner

Now that your questions are gently simmering on a back burner, you can move ahead and start cooking on the front burners. What is on those burners? The things you know to be true, despite the questions and circumstances. In the following chapters we'll take a look at some front-burner truths. At the close of each chapter there will be a Now Engage section that will invite you to meditate on the truths of God's Word—and to declare them out loud. This will build your faith and move you forward to victory.

Now Engage

It's OK to ask God your questions, but keep moving on to victory by declaring these truths from God's Word.

Front-Burner Truth: "I know it's OK to ask God my questions."

> Yea, though I walk through the valley of the
> shadow of death, I will fear no evil; for You are
> with me; Your rod and Your staff, they comfort me.
> —PSALM 23:4

I will not make a camp in the land of hurt, anger, or disappointment. I will keep walking *through* this valley. I'll ask my questions, put them on the back burner, and then keep moving forward with God. I am not afraid, because He is with me.

> I do not count myself to have apprehended; but
> one thing I do, forgetting those things which
> are behind and reaching forward to those things
> which are ahead, I press toward the goal for the
> prize of the upward call of God in Christ Jesus.
> —PHILIPPIANS 3:13–14

Just like the apostle Paul, with God's help I will forget those things that are behind and reach forward to the things that are ahead. I won't dwell on the past. I will *press* toward the things God has planned for my future. I will move forward with my life.

> Dear brothers and sisters, one final thing. Fix your
> thoughts on what is true, and honorable, and right,
> and pure, and lovely, and admirable. Think about
> things that are excellent and worthy of praise.
> —PHILIPPIANS 4:8, NLT

I am the CEO of my thoughts. I decide what I will think on, and I choose to fill my mind with good things. I choose to replace wrong thoughts with what God says in His Word. I will memorize Scripture, and when wrong thoughts come, I'll take those thoughts captive and think only about what God promises. I choose thoughts of joy and a good attitude.

"Happiness is something you
decide on ahead of time."

Chapter Two

HE'LL NEVER
LET YOU GO

WHEN YOU LEAVE your questions on a back burner and move your life to a front burner, you'll find God's plans for your life. You will also discover some truths about God—character traits and promises you can count on. One front-burner truth is that God will never leave you or forsake you. Not ever! This is something you can know, because He has promised it in His Word.

Hebrews 13:5 in the Amplified Bible puts it this way: "He [God] Himself has said, I will not in any way fail you nor give you up nor leave you without support. [I will] not, [I will] not, [I will] not in any degree leave you helpless nor forsake nor let [you] down (relax My hold on you)! [Assuredly not!]."

Don't you love that? Read it again—it is God talking to you.

You Are Safe

Whenever I read Hebrews 13:5, I picture a father teaching his three-year-old daughter how to swim. I see the dad in the water, extending his arms toward the little girl, who's at the edge of the pool looking down at him, very nervous about jumping in.

The dad says, "Go ahead and jump into the pool, honey. I'll catch you. I won't let go."

And full of faith that her daddy will catch her, the little girl jumps in and is scooped up by strong arms into a safe embrace. "I gotcha, honey, you're safe," her father says. He won't let go of her or relax his hold on her. Assuredly not!

That's how your heavenly Father is—He won't let go of you or relax His hold on you. Assuredly not! He's got you; you're safe, no matter how deep the water is.

When the foundation of my world was shaking, I read this verse in Hebrews over and over until it settled into my heart. There came a time when I knew that I knew that I knew that it was true *for me*: God had a firm hold on me; He would never let me go or give up on me.

God won't let go of you or
relax His hold on you.

How did I become so sure? By thinking on this truth. By meditating on it day and night, as the Bible instructs us to do.

> This Book of the Law shall not depart from your mouth, but you shall *meditate in it day and night*, that you may observe to do according to all that

is written in it. For then you will make your way
prosperous, and then you will have good success.

—JOSHUA 1:8,
EMPHASIS ADDED

I like the results this verse promises, don't you? When
you meditate on God's Word, you make your way prosperous and successful. *You* do it, because of your choice
to read and think on God's Word. You're in control. That
comes as really good news when circumstances feel as if
they're *out* of your control.

What does it mean to meditate? *Merriam-Webster's
Dictionary* definition is "to focus one's thoughts on:
reflect on or ponder over."[1]

Remember, you are the CEO of your thoughts. That
means you can decide what to think on. With your questions simmering away on a back burner, it's vital that
you take control of your thoughts and focus on God's
promises, which are found in His Word.

You can do that! Start by reflecting on Hebrews 13:5.
Don't just read the verse once and think, "Well, that
would be nice." Instead run it over in your mind again
and again. Read it out loud. Picture yourself being held
in God's strong arms. Hear Him saying this verse to *you*
and telling you what it means.

Spend more time thinking about what God has said
than you spend thinking about the troubles and questions all around you. (The Now Engage sections will
help you do just that.)

Meditating on the Word—giving it the most air-
time in your brain—is the secret to tapping into God's
freedom and power. It's the secret to putting the past

behind and moving on with Him. And you're the only one who can make that happen.

God Is on Your Side

Psalm 118:6 says, "The LORD is on my side; I will not fear." Despite any bad thing that may have happened in your life, God hasn't loosened His hold on you, and He's on your side! This means His power is *with you.*

There's a story in the Bible that illustrates this point. Second Kings 6 recounts how the king of Syria was at war with God's people, Israel. But God was quietly telling Israel's prophet Elisha the enemy's battle plans. As a result, Syria was repeatedly thwarted.

The king of Syria couldn't figure out how Israel's army was hearing about his plans in advance. At first, he suspected there was a spy. Then he discovered that Elisha was *eavesdropping* in the spirit!

As a result, the king of Syria purposed to hunt down Elisha. He found out where the prophet was staying and surrounded the place. When Elisha's servant looked out the window, he saw Syria's enemy army. He figured they were doomed and cried out to Elisha, "Alas my master! What shall we do?" (v. 15).

Elisha didn't panic. He didn't even get up to look out and see how vast the army was. No, Elisha had been listening so closely to the spirit of God that he knew what the king of Syria was saying in secret. He knew that God was with him and would protect him.

Elisha calmly told his servant, "Do not fear, for those who are with us are more than those who are with them" (v. 16). Then he prayed for his servant, "LORD, I pray, open his eyes that he may see" (v. 17).

In the spirit realm Elisha's servant saw a mountain that was full of horses and chariots of fire. It completely surrounded Elisha. Those horses and chariots of fire were sent by God to protect them.

God Sees Your Need

Elisha knew that there was more going on than met the physical eye. He saw the threat of attack from God's point of view. He knew in his heart that God had their back, because he was looking into the spirit realm, and he prayed that the servant could also see God's perspective.

God wants you to know that He is on your side, and He will never let you go. He wants your spiritual eyes to be open so you can see things from His point of view, not just in the natural. He is there, even when you cannot see Him. These things must be *seen* (discerned) in the spirit—in other words, by faith.

First Corinthians 2:9–10 says, "'Eye has not seen, nor ear heard, nor have entered into the heart of man the things which God has prepared for those who love Him.' But God has revealed them to us through His Spirit."

Your physical eyes and ears don't always see and hear what God is doing—those things have to be discerned by your spirit. But it is possible to hear His voice and follow Him. John 10:27 says, "My sheep hear My voice, and I know them, and they follow Me." Just as God revealed hope to Elisha's servant, He also wants to reveal to you that He's with you. He wants you to know that He won't let you go!

The way you come to believe this truth is by looking more into spiritual things than natural things. This kind of belief comes by reading and meditating on what He has said. When you believe His Word more than you believe what the circumstances around you tell you, then you have hope.

God Answers With a Miracle

A pastor's wife once told me about a woman in her church whose child had died at birth. Understandably that loss had broken the woman's heart. Unfortunately years after the loss it still tormented her, even though she had given birth to other children. She had camped out in the land of hurt and was stuck there.

Persuaded by her husband, the woman reluctantly attended church, but she didn't want anything to do with a God who would "steal her baby." Every time her pastors would say, "God is a good God," it would make her mad. All she could think was, "If He is good, why did my baby die?"

But then the woman's daughter became pregnant. The pastors and the church prayed with this young couple for a healthy, perfect baby. They believed for a smooth delivery. After a nearly flawless pregnancy, during the delivery it became evident that something was wrong. The placenta came out in pieces, and the umbilical cord was in shreds; however, the baby was *perfectly healthy and whole.*

With a damaged placenta and umbilical cord—the source of nourishment—the baby should have died in the womb. The doctors were amazed the child survived, and they called it a miracle.

The woman who had been camped in the land of hurt, still mourning over the loss of her own baby years before, finally realized that God *is* a good God. Yes, questions remained unanswered about her own loss, but now she could see that God had been working in the unseen realm on her daughter's and grandchild's behalf. He had performed a miracle not because of her faithfulness but because of His.

God is remarkable. Even if
you're mad at Him, He won't
give up on you. He won't turn
His back or walk away.

Second Timothy 2:13 says, "If we are faithless he always remains faithful" (PHILLIPS). I also like the way *The Message* renders this verse: "If we give up on him, he does not give up."

God is remarkable. Even if you're mad at Him, He won't give up on you. He won't turn His back or walk away.

Hebrews 10:23 says, "Let us hold fast the confession of *our* hope without wavering, for He who promised is faithful" (emphasis added). Rest assured, God is faithful. Even when something bad has happened and you have questions, He is faithful to His promises. He'll never let you go. You can hold fast to that.

He Will Take Care of You

I am convinced that a large number of Christians are not that sure of God. When they sit in church or when everything is going OK in their lives, they say, "God will take care of everything."

But when someone close to them dies or the doctor

gives them a bad report or they face financial problems or someone betrays them or they lose their job, then fear and doubt creep in. They begin to wonder, "Will God really take care of me?"

Of course, the answer is a resounding yes! God will take care of you—every time. But settling this front-burner truth in your heart is key to the very foundation of your faith. It will make all the difference in how bad situations will turn out in your life.

There is a wonderful story in the first chapter of Daniel that gives an excellent example of God's care for His people when they are in perilous situations.

In this story God's people, Israel, had just been carried off into captivity by the Babylonians because of their disobedience. Daniel and several other young men were chosen from the ranks of Israelite captives to be trained as leaders in King Nebuchadnezzar's Babylonian government.

As part of this group of elite candidates Daniel and his friends lived in the king's palace and were served delicious food that wasn't "kosher"—in other words, food that God had forbidden the Israelites to eat.

Daniel and three of his friends—Shadrach, Meshach, and Abednego—purposed in their hearts to obey God. The Bible says, "Daniel was determined not to defile himself by eating the food and wine given to them by the king. He asked the chief of staff for permission not to eat these unacceptable foods" (v. 8, NLT).

Now, if you think about it, declining food offered by the king takes a lot of guts. Even though Daniel and his three friends had been selected for government service, in reality they were really just glorified prisoners in the king's palace, which means they were expected to follow the king's orders. It might not seem wise for anyone in that position to say, "No, thanks" to *anything* served by their captors, even if they *were* chosen to be groomed for leadership.

Daniel wasn't only risking his own life, he was also endangering the king's chief of staff, the man in charge of all the trainees. When that man heard Daniel's request to abstain from eating the king's food, he replied, "I am afraid of my lord the king, who has ordered that you eat this food and wine. If you become pale and thin compared to the other youths your age, I am afraid the king will have me beheaded" (v. 10, NLT).

Daniel and his friends were under a lot of pressure as they chose to obey God. They obviously trusted that God would take care of them.

Daniel said to the chief of staff: "Please test us for ten days on a diet of vegetables and water.... At the end of the ten days, see how we look compared to the other young men who are eating the king's food. Then make your decision in light of what you see" (vv. 12–13, TLB).

Well, amazingly enough, the Bible says that these four young men looked *better* at the end of the ten days than the other candidates who ate the king's food. God supernaturally sustained them because they chose to believe Him. And as a result of their obedience under pressure, the Bible says that God rewarded them with knowledge and wisdom above everyone in the kingdom (vv. 15–20).

You Can Know

Daniel and his friends *knew* that God would take care of them—even when it looked like honoring Him would get them into trouble. After all, how big a deal would it have been to just eat the king's food? Many people would have chosen the path of least resistance in that case.

*God wants you to trust Him
so He can perform miracles
for you and promote you.*

But look what happened when they trusted God and chose His way. They received supernatural knowledge and wisdom (something everyone needs *all* the time). And it elevated them, even in the midst of their enemy's kingdom.

Think about that. Would you like to be elevated in the midst of your enemy's kingdom? The world is the enemy's kingdom, yet God can promote His children when they trust Him.

You can trust God to take care of you. He will never let go of you. Don't doubt Him! He wants you to trust Him so He can perform miracles for you and promote you, just as He did for Daniel and his three friends. You can have the same assurance they did when you keep your eyes on God's Word and believe Him.

He Is for You

The Book of Romans offers further reassurance that God is never going to let you go.

> If God is for us, who can be against us?...I am persuaded that neither death nor life, nor angels

nor principalities nor powers, nor things present
nor things to come, nor height nor depth, nor any
other created thing, shall be able to separate us
from the love of God.
—ROMANS 8:31, 38–39

This promise covers everything that has ever happened to you. *Nothing* can separate you from God's love.
He is for you. He will take care of you. He's never going
to let you go.

Now Engage

God will never leave you or forsake you—ever! Let this
truth sink deep within your spirit by meditating on and
declaring these truths from God's Word.

Front-Burner Truth: "I know God will never let go of me."

> He [God] Himself has said, I will not in any way
> fail you nor give you up nor leave you without sup-
> port. [I will] not, [I will] not, [I will] not in any
> degree leave you helpless nor forsake nor let [you]
> down (relax My hold on you)! [Assuredly not!].
> —HEBREWS 13:5, AMP

God will not fail me! He won't leave me helpless or
without His support. He has hold of me—He won't let
go. He won't ever let me down.

> This Book of the Law shall not depart from your
> mouth, but you shall meditate in it day and night,
> that you may observe to do according to all that

is written in it. For then you will make your way prosperous, and then you will have good success.

—Joshua 1:8

I will spend extra time reading and thinking on God's Word, day and night! I'll meditate on it instead of meditating on my questions or the things that have gone wrong. When I do that, I'm taking steps toward making my own way prosperous and insuring my good success.

The Lord is on my side; I will not fear.

—Psalm 118:6

I have no reason to be afraid. No matter what has happened in my life, God hasn't lost His hold on me, and He is on my side. That means the greater power is with *me*.

"Do not fear, for those who are with us are more than those who are with them."..."Lord, I pray, open his eyes that he may see."

—2 Kings 6:16–17

There is more going on here than meets the eye. I know in my heart that God has my back and that He is protecting me. I am going to spend more time "looking" into spiritual things than natural things by reading and meditating on His Word. Then my spiritual eyes will be open. I will believe the Word more than what I see all around me.

"Eye has not seen, nor ear heard, nor have entered into the heart of man the things which God has prepared for those who love Him." But God has revealed them to us through His Spirit.

—1 CORINTHIANS 2:9–10

I may not be able to see and hear right now what God is doing, but I believe He is revealing what I need to know by His Spirit. I hear His voice—He leads and guides me.

Let us hold fast the profession of our faith without wavering; (for he is faithful that promised).

—HEBREWS 10:23, KJV

My God is faithful! I will hold fast to that. Even when I have questions, I know that God honors His promises and that He will never let me go. He will keep working things out for me. I trust Him to do it—I believe He's doing it right now.

If God is for us, who can be against us?

—ROMANS 8:31

God is for me. He loves me! Nothing—nothing that has happened and none of my questions—can stand between Him and me.

Chapter Three

HE STILL HAS A GOOD PLAN

I N THE MOVIE *Home Alone* a little kid is left behind when his family goes on vacation at Christmastime. In one scene he pretends to be shaving, and when he's done, he applies aftershave by slapping his face with both hands—it hurts, so he yells, "Ahh!" In the movie trailer when we see that scene, it seems as if the little kid is freaking out because of being home alone with bad guys in the house.

As a result, whenever I think of someone in a panic or caught by surprise, I think of them slapping the sides of their face just as he did! I call it "making the *Home Alone* face."

Maybe something has happened in your life that has caught you completely by surprise, or makes you want to panic. Maybe you're making the "*Home Alone* face" (or you feel like making it) right now!

But there's one thing I want you to know: God is not on His throne making the *Home Alone* face, and He never will be. He never says, "Wow, I didn't see *that* coming!" The events of your life do not freak out God or catch Him by surprise. No matter what has (or has not) happened to you, another front-burner truth to focus on is: God still has a good plan for you.

Jeremiah 29:11 says, "I know what I'm doing. I have it all planned out—plans to take care of you, not abandon you, plans to give you the future you hope for" (THE MESSAGE).

I love this verse. It means that there *is* a plan for your life. You have a purpose for being here. That is a promise from God to you. And the plan hasn't changed. God knows the plan, and He wants to tell you all about it so that you can walk in it.

God's plan will produce good results in your life. I'm *glad* that the verse above says He knows what He's doing! You can trust Him. He has your best interest at heart.

He Is Not Surprised

You may have been stunned by something bad that has happened, but nothing ever surprises God. I was *really* surprised to find myself a widow at thirty-seven years of age, the single parent of two teenage boys, and senior pastor of a church.

Maybe you said the same thing about your situation— you might have been shocked by where you found yourself. Perhaps you asked, "How did I get *here*? This is *not* what I expected my life to look like!" When the unexpected happens, I hope that knowing God still has a plan for your life brings the same comfort to your heart as it did to mine. Whatever has happened (or hasn't happened) doesn't negate or change the plan. He still intends to carry it out.

My plan (or the way I thought my life was going to be) got blown out of the water, but God's plan did not. He's gone on to work that plan and purpose in my life and in the lives of my sons. It has turned out *far* better than anything we could have imagined or worked out ourselves. As I write this book, all three of us are serving God with all our hearts and working in full-time ministry. God has been so faithful to help us continue in His plan for our lives despite what we lost.

Second Timothy 1:9 declares that God has "saved us and called us with a holy calling." Every Christian is called to live a godly life, be a witness, grow up spiritually, walk in love with our brothers and sisters, and produce the fruit of the Spirit. You have an individual calling specific to your gifts and desires.

The calling of God doesn't change because something happens (or doesn't happen). It doesn't change because something catches us unaware. God is a good planner, and He sticks with a plan. Nothing derails Him.

Don't let the hard things, hurts,
questions, and disappointments
become more familiar to
you than your purpose.

Romans 11:29 says, "God's gifts and God's call are under full warranty—never canceled, never rescinded" (THE MESSAGE). Never! His call on your life is still the same, even after something happens, even if you have questions. It might not look like you expected, but it can be *even better* than you expect if you keep believing Him.

Ephesians 2:10 says, "We are His workmanship,

created in Christ Jesus for good works, which God prepared beforehand that we should walk in them." Before
you were born, God knew what you would be and do.
He prepared good works for you—things for you to be
and do.

Be encouraged—*keep* being and doing what God has
given you to be and do. Don't let the hard things, hurts,
questions, and disappointments become more familiar
to you than your purpose.

Jehovah Jireh Provides

When God has a plan, He's never worried about the outcome. He sees ahead and provides, which simply means
that He has prepared every detail in advance.

There is a story in Genesis 22 that clearly illustrates
God's foresight. In this story God asks Abraham to offer
his beloved son Isaac on the altar of sacrifice. This passage is packed with many wonderful teaching points.
I encourage you to read and study it. Right now I will
focus on the ram that God provided for the sacrifice so
that Abraham didn't have to kill Isaac.

As the story goes, when God asked Abraham to offer
Isaac, Abraham quickly obeyed. He took his son to
Mount Moriah and fully intended to kill him there (v. 10).
Abraham figured that if Isaac died, God could raise the
boy from the dead in order to fulfill His promise (Heb.
11:17–19).

At the moment Abraham was poised to plunge a knife
into Isaac, the Lord stopped him and said, "Do not lay
your hand on the lad, or do anything to him; for now I
know that you fear God, since you have not withheld
your son, your only son, from Me" (Gen. 22:12).

The following verses tell what happened next: "Then Abraham lifted his eyes and looked, and there behind him was a ram caught in a thicket by its horns. So Abraham went and took the ram, and offered it up for a burnt offering instead of his son. And Abraham called the name of the place, The-Lord-Will-Provide; as it is said to this day" (vv. 13–14).

This is the first place in the Bible where God is called Jehovah Jireh (v. 14, KJV), which means "the God who provides." It could even be interpreted as "the God who *sees ahead* and provides."

Think about all that transpired. God had sent Abraham to a mountain that was a three-day journey away from his home (v. 4). No doubt there were closer mountains. If I had been in Abraham's shoes, I might have said, "Lord, can't I just go over there to Mount Closer-to-Home and make this sacrifice there?"

But God had a plan and a provision. He could have sent a ram to any mountain, but for His reasons He had arranged for it to appear on Mount Moriah at the exact moment when Abraham would need it. If Abraham had pleaded for a more convenient mountain, he might have missed his provision. In the same way, today we might complain, "God, why do I have to go all the way *there* for school (or work, or church), when there's a perfectly good school (job or church) *right here* that I can go to?"

Be careful that you follow God's leading closely— because where He guides, He provides. You don't want to be in the wrong place at the wrong time with your provision waiting for you somewhere else.

Abraham knew how God's plan and provision worked. On that fateful day, while he was heading up one side of Mount Moriah, the ram was heading up the other side. He was in the right place at the right time. God *saw ahead* to what Abraham and Isaac would need, and He provided it.

Guess what? God has done the same for you. God has seen ahead in your situation and is providing exactly what you need. He was and always will be the God who sees ahead and provides.

Here Is Some More of My Own Story

After I had been pastor at our church in Boise for about four years, the Lord began to deal with me about moving back to Tulsa, Oklahoma, where both our sons had been born and where my husband had gone to Bible school in the early eighties.

I did not want to go! I winced at the idea of leaving the Northwest again and returning to the flat, hot Midwest. I did not want to move away from my natural family and my wonderful church family. I also did not want to go backward in my life after I had been in full-time ministry for more than fifteen years. I just didn't see how moving back to Oklahoma would be a promotion.

But God kept nudging me. When it's His idea, it sticks around. You can ignore Him for a while, or even try running away from Him, but He just keeps bringing you back to His original plan. That is why you can take your time to make sure you are following His lead. If it is God speaking today, it will still be God speaking next month or next year.

I will be honest. It took me awhile to get on board with God's plan. Because God kept prodding, I eventually had my sons (who by that time were seventeen and sixteen years old) pray too. As they listened to God, they agreed that the move was God's plan for us. With everyone finally on the same page, we sold our house, turned the church over to the associate pastor, and moved to Tulsa.

Following this part of God's plan was just about the scariest thing I had ever done, and it took all my faith. To make a long story short, I ended up getting a job as a writer at a private Christian university, and my working there enabled both my sons to attend that university for four years almost for free.

If you had told me five years earlier that I would be able to put two boys through a private university *by myself* at almost no cost, I would not have believed you. Yet God did that for us, because we chose to trust Him.

After a few years in Tulsa I got my dream job teaching at the Bible school where my husband had attended all those years before. It came in a way that only God could arrange, and I wouldn't have gotten that job if I hadn't been in the right place, serving faithfully where He had put me.

I found out that you cannot outdo God. He has a *good* plan, and if you'll stick with Him, He has a way to work the details out in your favor far beyond what you can imagine.

It May Go Differently Than You Expected

The years that I worked at the university were hard on me. I had been in the ministry full-time, and I had to go back to work as a writer, punching a clock and writing on demand for forty hours a week. Writing is what I had done *before* I went into ministry; it's my marketable skill.

Going back to it didn't feel like I was moving forward. It felt like a *demotion* not a promotion!

Going backward can really mess with your mind. It certainly wasn't what I expected for that season of my life. It didn't seem like the answer I had prayed for. I felt as if I had been relegated to the wilderness, like the children of Israel must have felt. It seemed that I had been forgotten, left behind. While all my ministry friends continued to preach, travel, lead churches, and change lives, I was stuck behind a desk again.

I call those four years "the cubicle years." I enjoyed the people I worked with, and my children greatly benefited from my time there by getting an almost free college education, but it was hard. I had to constantly keep my eyes on God's Word in order to keep from getting discouraged.

Based on Jeremiah 29:11 and Romans 11:29, I made this confession every day: "Father, I know You haven't forgotten about me or changed Your mind about me for one moment. *I will* fulfill Your plan for my life." I worked hard, stayed faithful in my church and at my job, and in the end God came through.

Sometimes things don't look like you expect them to look. You have questions. But that doesn't mean nothing is happening. God is always working when you trust Him.

Like me, you might get a different answer to your prayers than you expected. Can you trust Him? Does He still have a good plan and purpose for you? I believe that He does. But if you quit, you will never find out what it is. If you camp out in the land of hurt and questions, you will never get to your promised land.

My best advice is *keep going.* Your life may look

different now than you expected, but don't spend all your time looking back. Look forward. Be led by the Spirit, move when He says move, stay when He says stay, and be faithful and obedient. You never know when there is a ram headed up the mountain that will cross your path.

Go From Tragedy to Triumph

My friend Jeff Bardel is an example of someone whose life has gone in a different direction than he expected. Yet if you ask him, he will testify that despite tragedy, God's good plan has led him to triumph. Today he is more blessed than he ever could have imagined. He told me I could share his story with you.

In 1993 Jeff was working in a factory with his dad. He was eighteen years old, and it was the summer after he graduated from high school. Four days before his college orientation week was to begin, he was working at his factory job and suffered a horrible accident in which his right arm was torn off by a piece of machinery. Someone called an ambulance immediately, but before it arrived, Jeff died.

Jeff remembers leaving his body and looking down on himself lying in a pool of blood. When the paramedics did arrive, they were able to resuscitate him and rush him immediately to a hospital. There doctors operated, but while in surgery he died *again*.

Through heroic efforts, doctors were able to save Jeff's life one more time. But while he had hoped they'd be able to reattach the arm, when he awoke hours later in his hospital room, his right arm was gone—the doctors hadn't been able to save it.

I can't imagine what losing an arm would be like,

especially for a young man of eighteen. Not only did Jeff have to face life with a disability, but suddenly his boyhood dream was dashed. He had been an athlete with a promising baseball career in front of him. The loss must have been devastating.

Jeff questioned God, "Why did this happen? Why didn't You let me die?" To Jeff, life didn't seem to be worth living without a whole, healthy body. This certainly wasn't the life he had expected.

But Jeff didn't give up. He went to college, became a journalist, and then went to Bible school. He began to minister and share his testimony. Instead of focusing on his loss and everything that had gone wrong, he chose to focus on the good in his life. He believed he'd been given a second chance, and he didn't want to waste it.

To date, thousands of teens have been won to Christ through his ministry. And he didn't quit sports. Jeff took up golf, among other sports, and in 2006 he set the world record for the longest drive of a golf ball hit by a person with one arm. He has coached several sports teams, and he says his life has just gotten better and better.

Not long ago Jeff said something that encouraged me so much that I wrote it on a sticky note and stuck it on my computer monitor. He was looking back, first remembering how he had wanted his life to end after the accident, and then rejoicing over all God has done for him since the accident happened. He said, "No matter what's happening in your life today, there are plenty of great tomorrows in your future." Yes! It is true for Jeff, it is true for me, and it is true for you.

Keep Your Focus on the Outcome

When God starts on a plan, He doesn't get detoured. After all, He's God. You might think that a change in circumstances means the original plan will not happen, but circumstances are temporary and subject to change. Second Corinthians 4:18 says, "We do not look at the things which are seen, but at the things which are not seen. For the things which are seen are temporary, but the things which are not seen are eternal." Second Corinthians 5:7 says, "For we walk by faith, not by sight."

Don't believe more in the things you see today than you believe in God's plan for your life. Circumstances (good or bad) will change, but God's plan lasts. After all, it is eternal. You are wise to stay with Him and His plan, even when outward appearances look like you are on a detour.

Jesus kept His focus on God's purpose for His life. Look at Mark 4. Jesus stayed with the original plan despite adverse circumstances. After He had been teaching a huge crowd by the sea, Jesus wanted to leave. He loaded His disciples into a boat and told them, "Let us cross over to the other side" (v. 35).

Following through on the plan, Jesus and His disciples departed, and Jesus went to sleep in the back of the boat. But midway into the trip a huge storm came up, tossing the boat from side to side, threatening to sink it. The storm was so violent that the disciples, some of whom had been professional fishermen, were afraid for their lives.

Imagine the wind buffeting them, the waves lifting

and heaving the boat, the rain beating down until they couldn't see the shore. It had to have been frightening.

In a panic the disciples roused Jesus and shouted, "Master, don't you care that we're drowning?" (Mark 4:38, PHILLIPS). (You have to be pretty freaked out to wake up the Lord from His nap. I think I would be right there waking Him too! How about you?)

The storm didn't seem to bother Jesus at all. He had already declared what He planned would happen on this trip—He'd said, "Let's go to the other side," and that's what He meant. He foresaw the outcome, and He didn't waver because of circumstances. He didn't panic and say, "Uh oh, there's a storm." The storm didn't change a thing.

Spend more of your time thinking about His Word and your goals and less time worrying about the storm.

When the disciples woke Jesus, He simply got up, rebuked the wind, and said to the sea, "Peace, be still!" (v. 39). Then He rebuked *the disciples* for being afraid and not having faith (vv. 39–40). In other words Jesus chided them for moving off the original plan just because of circumstances. Because of the raging storm, they stopped focusing on what Jesus had said and gave their attention to the trouble that was afoot. It's easy to do that, isn't it?

This story should give you confidence. Jesus has a plan for your life. Sometimes storms come along—don't let them scare you or detour you. Don't be like the disciples, who thought the storm stopped the original plan.

Storms don't have anything to do with God working His plan. He foresees the outcome, so you can keep your eyes on it too. Keep believing Him.

You may have gone through a raging storm. Don't let it be the defining event of your life. Instead keep your focus on the Lord! Remember what He has told you. Remember the dreams in your heart that He has placed there, and keep moving toward them. Spend more of your time thinking about His Word and your goals and less time worrying about the storm.

This mind-set takes spiritual effort. When a storm hits, you have to decide to keep your questions on a back burner and keep God's promises on a front burner.

You can do it! Know this: God has a plan, and He's continuing with it. Stick to the plan. Trust Him to make your steps clear. Keep going to the other side—keep your eyes on the outcome.

Follow Jesus

When you are following God's plan for your life, it makes sense to follow someone who knows where He is going, someone who knows the way.

Of course, Jesus knows the way. In fact He told us in His Word that He *is* the way (John 14:6)! As you seek Him, the plan He has for your life will unfold. As you follow Him closely every step along the way, that plan will come into focus.

When you follow someone closely, you start following the way they think. Do you know some siblings, best friends, or married people who can finish each other's sentences? That comes from being together a lot and paying attention to each other.

You can choose to follow Jesus that closely. You can be together with Him by spending time reading and meditating on His Word or by praying. Following Him in this way will help you start thinking like He thinks. And I believe that when you start thinking like Jesus thinks, you can start living like Jesus lives. He is never worried, never sick, never in lack. I want to live like He lives. You can too.

Jesus knows the way to victory! He knows the way *through* the valley of shadows. He knows the way through the pain and the disappointments. I'm sure you'll agree that it's good to follow someone like that.

Despite the fact that Jesus knows the best way for you to go, He will never force you to follow Him. It is always going to be your choice.

One day some friends and I were going to a restaurant in a town that was several miles from where we lived. There were about twelve of us in the group, so we were in four cars, but not every driver knew the way. It was decided that we would follow our friend John, who was familiar with the area. All of us lined up behind John's car, that is, except for Carl, who *thought* he knew the way. In fact, Carl thought he knew a shortcut, so he decided to take it and beat the rest of us to the restaurant.

You can guess what happened. Carl chose not to follow John, who knew the way—and he got lost.

Much of the recovery and success of your life is up to you, especially after something horrible happens and you have questions. You get to choose. Joshua 24:15 says, "*Choose* for yourselves this day whom you will serve.... As for me and my house, we will serve the LORD" (emphasis added). Deuteronomy 30:19 quotes God as saying, "I call heaven and earth as witnesses today against you, that I have set before you life and death, blessing and cursing; therefore *choose life*, that both you and your descendants may live" (emphasis added).

We are the only ones who can decide what our attitude will be. We are the only ones who can decide to follow Jesus closely. Let's choose life! That is the way to victory and success.

There Is More to the Story

On the night my friends and I were headed out to eat, there was another friend, Gena, who *did* follow John's car. But on the way several vehicles not in our caravan pulled in between John and her. When the two lead cars arrived at the restaurant, Gena wasn't with us.

John called her cell phone and asked, "Where are you?" She replied, "I'm following you." She was following a car all right, but it wasn't John's car. Gena had been following John, but she wasn't following close enough to keep him in her sights. She ended up following the wrong car, so she lost her way.

If you have been a believer for a long time, then there have probably been some times when you were following Jesus more closely than other times. When you follow closely, things go better. When you're right up close to the One who created the universe and knows all things, your peace is greater, and your way is smoother. You go in the right direction.

Who gets to decide how close you stay to Jesus? You do!

It reminds me of an illustration I heard about a young couple. When this man and woman were dating, they drove around town in his pickup truck, which had a bench seat. If you were to drive up behind this couple on the street, you might think there was only one person in the truck, because the young lady was snuggled up so close to her sweetie that there was no space at all in between them. (*Ah*, young love!)

Several years went by. They got married, and pretty soon if you were to drive up behind them on the street, you would see the guy behind the wheel and his young wife all the way over next to the passenger door.

One day she said, "Honey, I just don't feel like we're as close as we used to be." The young man, holding onto the steering wheel, looked over at her and rather sadly asked, "Who moved?"

It is like that with Jesus and you. He is faithfully driving the car and will not move. Are you snuggled up close, or have you slid farther away? You get to choose.

Rest assured that God's good plan for your life is still in place. Do whatever it takes to follow Him as closely as possible.

Now Engage

No matter what has happened to you, God was not caught off guard. He still has a plan. Declare these truths over your situation and remind yourself that He still has you in the palm of His hand.

Front-Burner Truth: "I know God still has a good plan."

> I know what I'm doing. I have it all planned out—
> plans to take care of you, not abandon you, plans
> to give you the future you hope for.
> —JEREMIAH 29:11, THE MESSAGE

God is not surprised by where I find myself. There *is* a plan and purpose for my life. He knows what that plan is, and that is the future I hope for (it may be even better). Things are going to turn out well. God is leading and guiding me by His Spirit. I believe He knows what He's doing! I trust that He is bringing about the best possible outcome in my situation.

> [God] has saved us and called us with a holy calling.
> —2 TIMOTHY 1:9

Because I'm a Christian, I am called with a holy calling, and that doesn't change just because of the things that do or don't happen. God is sticking with His purpose and calling for my life, so I'm sticking with it too. I won't get derailed or give up.

> God's gifts and God's call are under full warranty— never canceled, never rescinded.
> —ROMANS 11:29, THE MESSAGE

God hasn't forgotten about me or changed His mind about me for a minute. His call on my life, the talents He has given me, and His plan and purpose for me are all still the same, no matter what has happened. My situation might not look the way I expected it to, but I'm going to believe that God can make things even better.

> [You] are His workmanship, created in Christ Jesus for good works, which God prepared beforehand that [you] should walk in them.
> —EPHESIANS 2:10

Before I was ever born, God knew what I would be and do. His plan and purpose for me are sure. He prepared things for me to do, so I'm going to do them.

> Then Abraham lifted his eyes and looked, and there behind him was a ram caught in a thicket by its horns. So Abraham went and took the ram, and offered it up for a burnt offering instead of his son. And Abraham called the name of the place, The-Lord-Will-Provide; as it is said to this day.
> —Genesis 22:13–14

My heavenly Father is Jehovah Jireh, the God who sees ahead and provides. Just as He saw ahead and provided the ram for Abraham, He has seen ahead in my life and is providing everything I need. Even if I can't see it yet, I trust that He is working right now on my behalf.

> We do not look at the things which are seen, but at the things which are not seen. For the things which are seen are temporary, but the things which are not seen are eternal.
> —2 Corinthians 4:18

I will not believe more in the things I see today than in God's plan. What I see in the natural (whether good or bad) will change, but God's plan is eternal. It won't change. I'll stay with Him—I'll walk by faith and not by sight.

> Let us cross over to the other side.
> —Mark 4:35

I'm going to keep moving forward with God's plan for my life, even when storms come along. I won't panic or be afraid of storms, because those circumstances are subject to change.

Chapter Four

YOU'RE NOT ALONE

SOMETIMES WHEN YOU are hurting and asking questions, you will feel very much alone. Maybe you feel like that today, like no one is standing with you. Maybe you feel as if you are facing the storms of life all by yourself.

One of the enemy's best lies is that no one understands what you're going through. Satan will try to convince you that no one cares. Believe it or not, he tells the same lie to anyone who will listen. At one time or another everyone has felt disheartened and abandoned.

But another front-burner truth that will bring hope in seemingly hopeless moments is this: no matter how you feel, you are *not* alone. You always have someone with you who sticks closer than a brother (Prov. 18:24). God is with you! And when He is with you, you can be sure that everything will turn out better than OK.

Follow the Guide on the Inside

Your heavenly Father is not a faraway God; He is a right-here-with-you God. Psalm 23 says He'll walk through the valley of the shadow of death *with* you. Matthew 1:23 calls Jesus "Immanuel," which means "God *with* us," not God far away from us. His very name declares His closeness.

It is easy to picture God on His throne *way* up there in heaven, *far away* from the problems here on earth. Indeed, God is seated on His throne in heaven, but He is also right inside you (John 14:17).

Your heavenly Father is not a faraway God; He is a right-here-with-you God.

When God-in-the-flesh (Jesus) was on earth, He said, "I will pray the Father, and He will give you another Helper, that He may abide with you forever" (John 14:16). I have news for you—Jesus prayed that before He left the earth, and the Father sent the Helper (the Holy Spirit) not long after Jesus departed (Acts 2). When you became a Christian, that Helper came to live in you forever.

John 14:16 in the Amplified Bible reads, "I will ask the Father, and He will give you another Comforter (Counselor, Helper, Intercessor, Advocate, Strengthener, and Standby), that He may remain with you forever." I love all of those adjectives! The Holy Spirit not only comforts you, but He also counsels and helps you, and He intercedes for you as a lawyer advocates for a client. He strengthens you and stands by you.

That makes me want to shout! This is the God who lives in you! You don't ever need to feel alone.

God meant it when He said the Holy Spirit would remain with you forever. Just think about forever. That means there is never a time you are outside His watchful care. He doesn't ever leave. You never go anywhere without Him. The psalmist wrote:

> Is there anyplace I can go to avoid your Spirit?
>   to be out of your sight?
> If I climb to the sky, you're there!
>   If I go underground, you're there!
> If I flew on morning's wings
>   to the far western horizon,
> You'd find me in a minute—
>   you're already there waiting!
> Then I said to myself, "Oh, he even sees me in the
>   dark!
>   At night I'm immersed in the light!"
>   —PSALM 139:7–12, THE MESSAGE

Even before Jesus came, when God's people were under the old covenant, God declared that He was watching over His children as a loving Father. How much more does that apply in His new covenant? Now Christians have His very Spirit living within them. When Jesus left the planet, He didn't leave His children hopeless and helpless. No, He left His Spirit!

> The Spirit of truth, whom the world cannot receive, because it neither sees Him nor knows Him; but you know Him, for He dwells with you and will be in you.
>   —JOHN 14:17–18

You know Him because He is with you and in you! And you have access to Him and all His power all day, every day. There is never a time when you are without His presence. Everything He is, everything He has access to, everything you need is right in your heart where the Holy Spirit dwells.

I like the way 2 Corinthians 12:9 is worded in the Amplified Bible: "My grace (My favor and loving-kindness and mercy) is enough for you [sufficient against any danger and enables you to bear the trouble manfully]; for My strength and power are made perfect (fulfilled and completed) and show themselves most effective in [your] weakness."

Did you get that? The times when you feel weak are the times when His strength is most effective. That is great news, because there are times when I feel weak. How wonderful to know that when I am weak, the Holy Spirit ends up looking His best.

Notice the Bible doesn't say, "C'mon! Buck up! Quit being weak!" God knows all about human emotions. No, He knew you would have times of feeling weak. So He put Someone inside of you to bolster you during those times. Basically He said, "Don't worry; when you're weak, I'm in there with My strength and power to show Myself strong. You're not alone."

There Are Other Helpers

Besides the fact that God Himself is always in you, always with you, He also assigns people to help you and pray for you. You may not even know some of them.

I once heard a story from a missionary who had been ministering in a foreign country many years ago.

In those days he and his ministry team traveled mostly by donkey along very rugged trails to remote villages in the mountains where most of the indigenous people had never heard the gospel or even seen a white person.

This missionary and his team members had made an agreement with one another that if any of them got sick or were unable to travel for any reason, the rest of the team would go on without the person who had fallen ill. They felt it was *that* important to reach this region with the good news.

One day this missionary got very sick. He couldn't ride his donkey and therefore couldn't continue with the team. As the team members had agreed to do, they left him in a remote village, even though no medical care was available.

After the team had moved on, the missionary got worse and worse. He knew that unless God intervened, he would die. As he grew weaker, it became harder and harder to pray for healing. On the third night he could only pray, "Father, help me." And he wondered if he would make it through the night.

As the sun came up the next morning, he was amazed to discover that not only was he alive, but also he was better. In fact, he got up from the mat where he had lain dying just the day before and ate some food. By the next day he was able to climb back on his donkey and eventually catch up with his ministry team.

But there is more to the story. Two years later this missionary was home on furlough in the United States, and while preaching in a church, he told the story of his miraculous healing. After the service a woman approached him and said, "Brother, may I ask you what was the date of your miraculously healing?"

The missionary checked his travel journal to see when he had been sick in the remote village. When he told the woman the date, she held up a journal of her own—it was her prayer journal. They compared entries and discovered that on *the exact date* two years earlier, when he had been lying on his deathbed, she had been awakened in the middle of the night by the Lord with an urgent directive to pray for someone in a foreign land.

Not only is God with you to
strengthen and help you...but
He is also enlisting the help
of others to pray *for* you.

Eager to obey, she prayed fervently for several hours, not stopping until she got a release and knew the prayer had been answered. Until that day when the missionary spoke at her church, she hadn't known who had needed intercession. When the missionary was too weak to pray for himself, God had arranged for someone else to hold him up in prayer.

Think about it. Right now God could be waking someone up in the night to pray for you. You are not alone. Not only is God with you to strengthen and help you in every situation, but He is also enlisting the help of others to pray *for* you.

Many People Prayed for Me

When my husband died, many people heard about it, and I know that many of them prayed for my sons and me. We needed the prayer. And we could feel the effects of it. I heard one story in particular several years later that amazed me.

In 2003 (about six years after Brent had died), both my sons were in college. Since they were old enough to care for themselves, I was able to go on a missionary trip to Romania that was organized by my church in Tulsa. This was one of my first overseas ministry trips. There were about fifteen people on the ministry team, and on the flight over I sat next to a team member I had never met before this trip.

At one point on our flight the gentleman said to me, "Actually I've known about you and your sons for a long time." He went on to explain that six years earlier he and his wife were attending a church in a neighboring state when they had heard about Brent's death. The Lord had laid it on the hearts of this man and his family to pray for us—for three years!

Can you imagine? A family we didn't know interceded for my boys and me for three years. And I didn't find out about it until six years later.

When you are at your weakest, God makes provision to have others help. The helpers could live in the same town or around the world. It doesn't matter. What matters is that they are praying. You are not alone. God is with you, and so are others.

You Are Never Alone

I travel and minister all over the country and around the world now. As I go, often I have had people say to me, "You go all those places alone? Aren't you scared?" I always reply, "Oh, I'm not alone. The Holy Spirit and all the angels go with me every step of the way. It's a crowd everywhere I go!" The same is true for you.

Besides promising that the Holy Spirit will always be with you and enlisting the help of other saints when you need them, God has promised that His angels will be with you too! Psalm 91:11–12 says, "For he will order his angels to protect you wherever you go. They will hold you up with their hands so you won't even hurt your foot on a stone" (NLT). You are not alone. You have supernatural guards around you all the time!

Despite what Hollywood has tried to tell us, angels are not mere humans who have earned their wings. Humans and angels are different kinds of beings, and they don't morph into each other or change places (Ps. 8:4–5). Angels are powerful heavenly beings, carrying out the works of God on earth and in the spirit realm.

Hebrews 1:14 says, "Are they [angels] not all ministering spirits sent forth to minister for those who will inherit salvation?" Human beings who accept Christ as Savior are the heirs of salvation (Rom. 8:17). So according to the Word, angels are sent forth to minister *to you*.

How many angels are available? Using Isaiah 14:12–14 and Revelation 12:3–4 as guidelines, most scholars agree that a third of the angels fell from heaven with Lucifer (Satan) and became demons. That means that two-thirds of the angels remained in heaven and serve God. That means there are twice as many angels on our side! These angels are waiting to protect you and me. They live to carry out our bidding according to the Word of God.

Just between you and me, I have a feeling that most Christians don't know this, so they aren't tapping them as a resource. In my mind this means that there may very well be a lot of angels standing around with nothing to do! Why not just go ahead and use them to protect you and carry out God's Word in your life? What do you think?

Just remember, you're not alone. You have the Holy Spirit in you, and He'll never leave you or forsake you. You have countless angels at your command. And you have other people praying for you. That's a lot to be encouraged about—you are a crowd wherever you go!

Now Engage

You are never alone. God is always with you. Meditate on and declare these promises from God's Word to build your confidence in the truth that God will never leave you and things will turn out better than OK.

Front-Burner Truth: "I know I'm not alone."

> "Behold, the virgin shall be with child, and bear a Son, and they shall call His name Immanuel," which is translated, *"God with us."*
>
> —MATTHEW 1:23,
> EMPHASIS ADDED

I'm not alone. Jesus is with me! His very name, Immanuel, says so. And because He is with me, things are turning out better than OK. My heavenly Father is not far away from everything I'm dealing with. He's a right-here-with-me God, so I'm not afraid.

> I will ask the Father, and He will give you another Comforter (Counselor, Helper, Intercessor, Advocate, Strengthener, and Standby), that He may remain with you forever.
> —JOHN 14:16, AMP

The Holy Spirit comforts, counsels, and helps me, intercedes for me like a lawyer, strengthens me, and stands by me! He lives right inside me, and He will stay with me *forever.* That means there's never a time when I am outside His watchful care. I never go anywhere without Him.

> My grace (My favor and loving-kindness and mercy) is enough for you [sufficient against any danger and enables you to bear the trouble manfully]; for My strength and power are made perfect (fulfilled and completed) and show themselves most effective in [your] weakness.
> —2 CORINTHIANS 12:9, AMP

The times when I feel weak are the times when God's strength is *most* effective. He knew I'd have times of weakness, so He put the Holy Spirit inside me to bolster me up in those times. He is in me with His strength and power to show Himself strong when I need Him. I am never alone.

For he will order his angels to protect you wherever you go. They will hold you up with their
hands so you won't even hurt your foot on a stone.
—Psalm 91:10–12, nlt

According to God's Word I have supernatural guards
around me all the time. God's angels—His powerful
heavenly beings—are ministering to me and for me, carrying out the works of God in the earth and in the spirit
realm.

Chapter Five

ONE THING
NEVER CHANGES

I N THIS WORLD everything changes. Governments change, buildings change, people change, you change, I change. Countries, prices, social norms, icebergs, music, and even mountains all change!

Think about the Constitution of the United States. Growing up in America, I learned that when the Constitution was written by the Founding Fathers in 1787, it was essentially the beginning of our nation. The Constitution is our foundation, the highest law in the land. All other laws must be compatible with the Constitution. It is the main document that sets up the workings of the federal government.

But even something as solid and lasting as the Constitution has changed since it was created. There have been twenty-seven amendments (changes) to the constitution. The most recent change, the twenty-seventh amendment, was adopted in 1992.

Obviously if there's one constant in this life, it's change. But amid all of this change one thing remains constant, and that is God. Malachi 3:6 says, "I am the

LORD, I change not." Hebrews 13:8 says Jesus is the same "yesterday, today, and forever."

Lots of circumstances may have changed in your life, but a front-burner truth is this: your covenant with God, bought by the blood of Christ, will never change. His love and care for you will be constant.

When everything else shifts and changes, you remain standing on a solid foundation. Hebrews 7:24–25 says, "But He [Jesus], because He continues forever, has an unchangeable priesthood. Therefore He is also able to save to the uttermost those who come to God through Him, since He always lives to make intercession for them."

Look at all of the words that provide hope in that verse: *forever, unchangeable, uttermost, always.* There is no room for doubt. In a world that is constantly changing, the One who saved you never changes.

Stand on the Rock

When my husband died, it felt as if the world all around me was sinking sand. Maybe you have been in that place too—maybe you are there now. The bottom has fallen out. Nothing seems sure. Your very foundation has been shaken. But there is a place to stand, a rock to firmly hold on to that won't move or shift. That rock is God. He is faithful, and His promises are yes and amen (2 Cor. 1:20).

What is a rock? It is a symbol of something solid and immoveable. Imagine yourself standing on a big rock in the middle of a field during a storm. Clouds race across the sky and a fierce wind whips through the grass and the trees. Pieces of paper, cardboard, and foliage sail by. Lightning cracks and thunder roars.

It seems as if everything is being tossed around in the wind, except you. You are standing on the rock. The rock isn't moved by the storm. It is staying in the same place, strong and firm. When the storm ends, you will still be standing there too, because your rock didn't budge.

First Corinthians 10:4 refers to Jesus as a Rock. In Luke Jesus said, "Whoever comes to Me, and hears My sayings and does them, I will show you whom he is like: He is like a man building a house, who dug deep and laid the foundation on the rock. And when the flood arose, the stream beat vehemently against that house, and could not shake it, for it was founded on the rock" (Luke 6:47–48).

In these verses you can see that a house that is built on a rock is established; it is grounded. When the storms of life come (which they always do), if your house is built upon this rock, it will remain standing. Another reference to the rock is found in Matthew. Jesus asked His disciples, "Who do you say I am?" (Matt. 16:15). Peter answered, "You are the Christ" (v. 16). To that Jesus said, "Blessed are you, Simon Bar-Jonah, for flesh and blood has not revealed this to you, but My Father who is in heaven. And I also say to you that you are Peter, and on this rock I will build My church, and the gates of Hades shall not prevail against it" (vv. 17–18).

The word *rock* in this verse is referring to the rock-solid revelation that Peter had regarding who Jesus really is. There were plenty of people who saw Jesus and His miracles, but not all of them understood that He was the Messiah for whom they had been waiting, the Son of God who had come to save the world from sin. Peter *did* understand this truth, and God built His church on this powerful, immoveable understanding.

In Christ you are standing on a solid rock, an unchanging foundation. The gates of hell cannot prevail against you. Nothing moves or changes God. That is good news in the midst of our ever-changing world. He is a solid rock on which you can build your life.

Jesus Is Still the Same

No matter what changes come about in your life, God remains the same. He continues to do what He's always done. He still saves, heals, delivers, and loves you. He still watches over you and orders your steps. His purposes for you and for mankind haven't been altered.

What are God's purposes? When you have questions, I think it's especially important for you to know that His purposes haven't wavered. You will have ups and downs, but you need to keep your focus on God's purposes and be useful in His kingdom. That is living on a front burner.

God's primary purpose is to rescue sinners, and He's still doing that today. Luke 19:10 says, "The Son of Man has come to seek and to save that which was lost." Matthew 20:28 says, "The Son of Man did not come to be served, but to serve, and to give His life a ransom for many." Jesus came to lay down His life for you, for me, and for every other human on this planet. Even if your world has come to a grinding halt, Jesus hasn't stopped acting like Jesus. Not for one minute. He came to bring mankind back into fellowship with Almighty God, and He's still doing so today and every day.

The gospel hasn't changed. It is still good news. And it

is available to everyone. Jesus said, "And I, if I am lifted up from the earth, will draw *all peoples* to Myself" (John 12:32, emphasis added). Nobody is excluded. Everyone can freely come and receive all Jesus is and all He has. This truth hasn't changed.

After salvation, God's next purpose is to fill Christians with His Holy Spirit. The Book of Acts records five times when new believers are filled with the Spirit (Acts 2:4; 8:15–18; 9:10–18; 10:34–38; 19:1–6). Just because those examples happened years ago doesn't mean this purpose of God is only in the past. There is nothing in Scripture that suggests baptism in the Spirit has ceased. Just the opposite is true: God wants all believers to have this power (Acts 1:8).

What a wonderful gift God has given to us in the Holy Spirit. The Bible says that, among other benefits, the Holy Spirit can edify you (Jude 20), guide you (Rom. 8:14), and help you pray when you don't know what to pray (Rom. 8:26). No wonder He wants you to be Spirit-filled.

God's purposes don't end there. He wants born-again, Spirit-filled believers to grow up spiritually. This has been His intention from the beginning, and He hasn't changed His mind. Becoming mature believers is what much of the New Testament is all about. Ephesians 4:14–15 says, "That we should no longer be children, tossed to and fro and carried about with every wind of doctrine, by the trickery of men, in the cunning crafti-ness of deceitful plotting, but, speaking the truth in love, may *grow up* in all things" (emphasis added).

When we are born again, we are baby Christians. There is nothing wrong with being a baby—we all started that way. But God doesn't want any of us to remain babies.

Babies can't do much for themselves, which means that they require a lot of care from someone else. Like any good father, God wants us to grow up and live productive lives. That is why He has given us instructions for growth.

None of these primary purposes have changed. God is still focused on them. It is important for us to stay focused on them as well.

He Is Your Refuge

Here's another thing that hasn't changed: your heavenly Father has promised to protect and hide you from trouble. Psalm 91:2 says, "I will say of the LORD, 'He is my refuge and my fortress; My God, in Him I will trust.'" Even in the midst of the storms of life, this is His Word to you. It's more sure and more lasting than the storms that may be swirling all around you.

Take a look at that psalm again. A refuge and a fortress are not temporary shelters. They remain. You can count on them. A refuge and shelter are what your heavenly Father is for you. Proverbs 18:10 says, "The name of the LORD is a strong tower; the righteous run to it and are safe." The name of Jesus is the completion of all the names of Jehovah, our God. When you say "Jesus," you have said it all: He is healer, provider, banner, prince of peace, and more. I love this picture of the name of Jesus as our strong tower. It goes right along with the image of Him as a fortress, a strong place of refuge.

God is trying to show us something here. When an enemy or a storm is raging against you and you have questions, there is no safer place to be than in the refuge of a strong tower. That tower isn't going to get blown over or blown up; it is going to stay standing with you safely inside.

Everyone needs a safe place to run to. God is your safe place, and He is *strong.* If you are a Christian, you are "the righteous" one this proverb is talking about, so go ahead and run into this place of refuge that has been provided for you! When you use the name of Jesus, you run into your strong tower, and you are safe.

My pastor once told a story about how the name of Jesus keeps us safe. When he was a small boy, he would stay at his grandmother's house. This was during the Great Depression when a lot of people were out of work and hungry. Many people were desperate and would do anything to obtain money to feed themselves or their families.

There was a rumor in the town where his grandmother lived that she had a big chest full of money hidden in her house. I can't remember how the rumor got started, but the truth was, all she had in that big chest were quilts and blankets. Still, the rumor persisted.

One night when my pastor was staying with his grandmother, he heard some noise coming from outside the house. He quickly alerted his grandmother, and the two of them hid. From behind the sofa, where they were crouched, they watched a nearby window as a man jimmied its lock and then raised it. They recognized the man who was trying to break in as someone in their town who was very poor and out of work.

My pastor was scared and didn't know what to do, but his grandmother calmly placed her hand on his shoulder and began to whisper, "Jesus, Jesus, Jesus." As she repeated the name of Jesus, the man kept trying to get in. He put his leg over the windowsill, but it just wouldn't go through the open space. He lifted his leg up and pushed his foot toward the opening, but it seemed to hit an invisible barrier. Eventually he stopped trying, slid the window back down, and walked away, shaking his head and muttering.

For my pastor and his grandmother the name of Jesus was literally a shield, a strong tower where they were safe from the intruder. Psalm 46:1 says, "God is our refuge and strength, a very present help in trouble." God is right there with you when there's trouble.

I have often found God to be my refuge and my strength. When I draw near to Him, He always draws near to me, and He will draw near to you too (James 4:8). That truth never changes.

A Lot Can Change

When my husband died, it wasn't just one thing that changed in our lives; a hundred things changed. To begin with, I wasn't a wife anymore. Often when I talk with other widows, I notice we all have the same question, even if we word it in different ways. We ask, "I *was* a wife. What am I *now*?" It is a scary question, and it took me a while to figure out the answer.

Women especially, it seems, spend much of their waking hours thinking about others. They think about their husbands, kids, jobs—everyone except themselves. Then when we lose a significant role, whether the loss comes through death, divorce, or other ways, we are no longer sure who we are.

My becoming a widow wasn't the only thing that changed in our family. Suddenly my sons went from having a father to *not* having one. There was no longer anyone to play football with them at the neighborhood park or to play basketball in the driveway. No one was there to have heart-to-heart, father-and-son talks. There was a void.

The situation changed at our church too. Our pastor wasn't there anymore to take care of the people, preach the sermons, or shake hands at the door after service. Pastor Mom had to do all that now. Taking on my husband's pastoral duties was an adjustment in itself, but it also raised the question of who would do all the things that Mom used to do at home?

You get the picture. There were a lot of changes and adjustments. Perhaps you can identify.

Go Through the Grieving Process

If you're asking questions because you've lost a loved one, a relationship, a job, or something similar, you need to go through a grieving process. There *is* a valley of the shadow of death or loss, as Psalm 23 says.

When you've lost something substantial, it takes some time to adjust. It is as simple as that. You have to say good-bye to the way things were, but this transition doesn't happen overnight.

Too often people try to push down the feelings and emotions that come during the grieving process. That's not healthy, because the feelings will surface later on. It is OK to be sad when you lose something. It is permissible to cry. In fact, tears are cleansing, and you'll never be able to get on with life until you cry—sometimes a lot.

I'm not an expert on grieving, but there are lots of good materials available on the subject. I like to recommend a great book my friend Rev. Tony Cooke wrote titled *Life After Death* (www.tonycooke.org) that has helped many people who are going through a loss. Whatever resources you choose, please pick some up, as they will help you through your pain. I do have some experience with grieving, and I've talked with many other people who have also gone through the process. Everyone who suffers loss goes through some basic stages of grief, including denial, guilt, anger, depression, reconstruction, and acceptance. It's good to know about these stages, in part so you know you're normal.

Each person will work through the stages in different ways and with different timing. You may fly through a couple of the stages and then take longer to process through another. Don't let anyone try to tell you how long it should take or that you're doing it wrong.

I once spoke with a gentleman who had lost his wife to cancer six months earlier. He wept as he told me about a letter he had received from a family member, telling him that it was high time he got rid of his wife's clothing and pictures and moved on with his life. He said, "Is that right, Miss Karen? Is it high time?"

No matter how well meaning people are, they aren't you. They cannot possibly go through your particular valley, and they don't know exactly what you're feeling. The process for each person and each loss will be different. I told this gentleman that if he wasn't ready to get rid of his wife's clothing, then he didn't have to. There are no rules about how long each step of the process should take. Everyone is different.

On the other hand, if having his wife's clothing around was making him depressed, then he might need to rethink things. Sometimes it's just too hard to handle the presence of a loved one's belongings because of the memories they stir. If having these things around weighs on you, then it's time for them to go. If it's too hard for you to do it yourself, then consider getting someone else to help remove them.

When my husband died, I tried to keep our surroundings the same, as much as was possible. I did this for my sake and for the sake of my sons. We stayed in the same house, went to the same schools, and attended the same church. We kept the same basic routine. It's often said that you shouldn't make any major decision or change for a year after losing someone close.

On the other hand, I had a friend whose husband died just a few months before mine did. They were a little bit older, so their kids were grown and out of the house, and they had just finished building their dream home. After her husband died, she lived alone and the house became like a prison to her. It was too big for one person, and she became sad every day because he wasn't there to enjoy it with her. So she moved. For my sons and me, staying in the same place was the right answer. For my friend, moving was the right answer.

Give yourself time. This is important whether you're recovering from the death of someone close, a divorce, a breakup, or any other kind of loss. Get around other people. Join a support group. Be sure to get yourself outdoors as often as possible. Breathe fresh air and feel the sunshine. Each day do something that you love. Pamper yourself for a while.

Everyone has different needs depending on the situation and dynamic. If you lose a job or have a sudden physical setback, moving may not be the big question, but there may be another dilemma. Do what seems best for you.

Through my greatest trial I learned how fragile life is. I became determined to live it to the fullest. While my husband was alive, I was a bit of a list person. By this I mean that I always had a long list of tasks and goals. I bulldozed my way through life with my to-do list, often missing the special moments and the special people that make life sweet.

My need to have all my ducks in a row came to light after Brent was gone, and I changed my ways. You have no doubt heard the phrase, "Stop and smell the roses." It means, "Stop barreling through life! Make yourself pause for a minute and savor the sweet things."

I love roses, so I literally made it a habit not only to repeat that saying over and over again but also to live it out. Anyone who has been around me knows that now whenever I see a rose, I stop and smell it. It's my rule! It's just one way that I remind myself to be present in the moment, to enjoy every little blessing that God sends my way.

When you're recovering from loss, there will be good days and bad days. You need to accept that. Enjoy every sweet moment that comes along, even if they're few and far between, and press through the bad moments. Believe that tomorrow will be better. I promise, if you keep going and don't camp out in the land of loss and pain, some day you *will* feel like yourself again. You aren't like those who sorrow without hope (1 Thess. 4:13). There is an end to the horrible feeling of loss and sadness.

I like Psalm 30:5: "Weeping may endure for a night, but

joy comes in the morning." God doesn't mind if you cry! Crying is good for you. It is a release. It is natural to cry when you suffer a loss. You can cry and still believe that God is good and that He will see you through, because part of standing in faith is knowing that morning *will* come! Grieving doesn't mean you're weak. You just don't want to get stuck in the grieving process or let a *spirit* of grief settle into your life.

I believe the best way to avoid that is to do what we've been talking about so far: ask your questions, put them on the back burner, and then keep "cooking" on the front burners of your life by doing what you know to do. Keep moving forward with God, because He never changes even when everything else does.

God Is Good

When something horrible happens, it is easy to become confused, especially when you start wondering who or what caused it. Too many people, even Christians, think that God was the cause, or at the very least, He stood by and allowed it to occur.

There is something I have to get straight right now: *God is good, and the devil is bad.* And that never changes. If you remember nothing else from this book, please remember that!

God did not cause your trouble. He did not steal from you, nor did He kill anybody. He didn't stand idly by and allow your trauma to happen. What kind of Father would do that? Only a cruel, abusive, untrustworthy father would allow something bad to happen to his child. God is none of those things! He's not schizophrenic either.

He doesn't do good one moment and then do bad the next. He is a good and loving Father.

Who then is at the root of evil on the earth? We have an enemy, and it is Satan. In John 10:10 Jesus calls Satan "the thief," and He says, "The thief does not come except to steal, and to kill, and to destroy. I have come that they may have life, and that they may have it more abundantly."

> There is something I have to get straight right now: *God is good, and the devil is bad.*

This verse clearly states the role of the devil and the role of Jesus—and the two never switch. The devil steals, kills, and destroys. It's his job, and he does it well. If someone stole your loved one, money, or peace of mind, it was the devil, not God.

Jesus came to bring you abundant life. That's *His* job. First John 1:5 says, "God is light and in Him is no darkness at all." He has no capacity for darkness, only light.

James 1:17 adds, "Every good gift and every perfect gift is from above, and comes down from the Father of lights, with whom there is no variation or shadow of turning." In other words, only good comes from God. He won't change from good to bad.

He is not sometimes saving and then sometimes killing. Satan is the ruler of the darkness—the one who is stealing, killing, and destroying on this earth. That is why the Bible says when you got saved you passed from darkness to light. (See Acts 26:18; 2 Corinthians 4:6.) You moved from Satan's kingdom into God's kingdom. In the Bible light is an attribute of God; darkness is an attribute of the enemy.

One of the biggest lies the devil tells people is that God causes bad things to happen—because the devil knows that if he can get you to blame God or make you doubt God, then He has cut you off from your help. He has stopped you from trusting the One who loves you and still has a good plan for you. He has stopped your faith cold.

If the devil succeeds in getting you to believe that lie, then hopelessness sets in. Don't listen to that liar! Don't believe that God has stolen anything from you or caused something bad to happen to you.

Make no mistake about it, and don't ever get confused again. God is *good.* You may have questions and may not understand why some things happen, but that doesn't change the nature of your heavenly Father. His intention and attention toward you are always good and only for your good.

Look at what the Bible says:

> Oh, taste and see that the LORD is good; blessed is the man who trusts in Him!
> —PSALM 34:8

> For the LORD is good; His mercy is everlasting, and His truth endures to all generations.
> —PSALM 100:5

> Praise the LORD, for the LORD is good.
> —PSALM 135:3

> The LORD is good to all, and His tender mercies
> are over all His works.
>
> —PSALM 145:9

I pray that you would clearly see this truth: God is good all the time, and He will never change. Don't run from Him or blame Him, even when you have questions. He is your refuge and strength. You're blessed when you trust Him. He is very trustworthy, and His tender mercy toward you is everlasting. He only wants the best for you.

Recognize Your Enemy

The reason that evil things happen, even to Christians, is because, according to the Bible, Satan is the ruler of this planet, not God. God created the earth for mankind, and He turned the rule over to us. As He was creating Adam, He said, "Let Us make man in Our image, according to Our likeness; *let them have dominion* over the fish of the sea, over the birds of the air, and over the cattle, over all the earth and over every creeping thing that creeps on the earth" (Gen. 1:26, emphasis added).

After God created Adam and Eve, He blessed them and told them to take dominion over everything on the earth (vv. 27–31). He just gave them one condition: "And the LORD God commanded the man, saying, 'Of every tree of the garden you may freely eat; but of the tree of the knowledge of good and evil you shall not eat, for in the day that you eat of it you shall surely die'" (Gen. 2:16–17).

The problem started when the serpent (Satan) tempted Eve to eat the fruit of the one tree that God had forbidden them to eat (Gen. 3). Up to that time Adam and

Eve had total dominion of the garden, and they had a perfect relationship with God. They obeyed Him, and His blessing was fully upon them.

But the serpent said to Eve, "Did God really say you must not eat of the fruit from any of the trees in the garden?" (Gen. 3:1, NLT). She replied, "We may eat the fruit of the trees of the garden; but of the fruit of the tree which is in the midst of the garden, God has said, 'You shall not eat it, nor shall you touch it, lest you die'" (vv. 2–3).

Satan responded by doing what he often does, he mixed a little bit of truth in with a lie. He said to Eve, "You won't die!...God knows that your eyes will be opened as soon as you eat it, and you will be like God, knowing good and evil!" (vv. 4–5, NLT). It was true that she wouldn't fall to the ground right then and die. But she would die spiritually, just as all mankind would after her.

You know what happened next. She ate the fruit. And she offered a piece to Adam, who ate too. The Bible tells the result of their act: "Then the eyes of both of them were opened, and they knew that they were naked; and they sewed fig leaves together and made themselves coverings" (v. 7). For the first time they hid in shame from God.

By this act of disobedience mankind died spiritually, sin entered the world, and dominion of the earth was turned over to the enemy (Rom. 5:12–15). God explained to Adam the result of this disobedience:

> Cursed is the ground for your sake; in toil you shall
> eat of it all the days of your life. Both thorns and

> thistles it shall bring forth for you, and you shall
> eat the herb of the field. In the sweat of your face
> you shall eat bread till you return to the ground,
> for out of it you were taken; for dust you are, and
> to dust you shall return.
> —GENESIS 3:17–19

As you can see, one man's sin (Adam's) brought a curse on this world. Thank God that one man's sacrifice (Jesus's) made redemption from the curse possible when a person accepts Him as Lord. "Just as one trespass resulted in condemnation for all people, so also one righteous act resulted in justification and life for all people" (Rom. 5:18, NIV).

Even though Jesus has come to redeem *mankind* (Gal. 3:13), the *world* still lives under the weight of sin's curse. Second Corinthians 4:4 says that Satan is still the god of this world. You only have to look around or watch the evening news to see how absolutely true that is. There is stealing, killing, and destroying going on all around us.

Through Jesus you have been redeemed from the curse (Rom. 3:24), but the earth has not. This truth explains why so many bad things happen.

As a redeemed being you can live *above* the curse, as long as you use your authority in Christ. Colossians 2:15 says of Jesus, "Having disarmed principalities and powers, He made a public spectacle of them, triumphing over them in it." Luke 10:19 tells how Jesus gave authority back to mankind: "Behold, I give you the authority to trample on serpents and scorpions, and over all the power of the enemy, and nothing shall by any means hurt you."

By defeating Satan (1 John 3:8), Jesus gave anyone

who believes in Him spiritual authority over the devil. You just need to enforce it. This means that instead of allowing the curse to run over your life, you must resist the devil. James 4:7 says, "Therefore submit to God. Resist the devil and he will flee from you." Notice that he *will* flee from you. You are the one with the authority. Jesus gave it to you, and He never changes.

What does it mean to have authority? Don't confuse authority with strength. You don't have to possess the physical strength to defeat your enemy; you simply need the spiritual authority that has already been given to you in Christ. For example, a city policeman standing in the street can stop an eighteen-wheeler semitruck by simply holding up his hand. Of course, he is not stopping that truck with his own *strength*. He is stopping it because he is backed by the *authority* of the city, and the driver of the truck recognizes that authority.

> If you think God is the cause of trouble and evil...then you won't recognize when the devil is at work, and you will not know to resist him.

In the same way, when you resist the devil by using the name of Jesus, the devil has to flee. He must run not because of *your* strength but because you're backed by the authority of heaven. However, this works only if and when you use your authority. You have to enforce the devil's defeat by resisting.

In order to use your authority over the devil, you have

to recognize him. You have to know your enemy. You cannot be confused about what comes from God and what comes from the devil. If you think God is the cause of trouble and evil, or if you think He flip-flops back and forth from good guy to bad guy, then you won't recognize when the devil is at work, and you will not know to resist him. If you don't use your authority to resist, the curse may be able to run right over you.

It is important that you understand who your enemy is. Your adversary is not God or other people. Your foe is the thief, the devil, the one whose job it is to steal, kill, and destroy. That is never going to change.

God Teaches You

Maybe you've heard people say, "God's put this trouble/trial/sickness on you to teach you something." Or maybe someone's well-meaning advice went like this: "God has allowed this trouble/trial/sickness to come upon you to help you grow."

That simply isn't true! It may sound spiritual to say something like that, but it is wrong. Remember, God never changes, and He is always good. I know that I am repeating this truth, but it's so important that you understand it.

Sometimes people say that Paul's thorn in the flesh in 2 Corinthians 12:7 was given by God. But look closely at that verse. Paul said, "And lest I should be exalted above measure by the abundance of the revelations, a thorn in the flesh was given to me, a messenger of Satan to buffet me, lest I be exalted above measure." It clearly says that the thorn was "a messenger of Satan," not of God! Don't be confused – God isn't using Satan's messengers in any of His dealings with us, His children!

Consider sickness as an example. Some people say God put sickness on them to teach them something. If this is true, then they're saying that it is *God's will* that they are sick, right? Yet these same people take medicine or go to the doctor to try and get the illness to go away.

I want to say to them, "Wait a minute. If the sickness is God's *will* for you, if this is how He's going to train and teach you, then why are you going to the doctor and trying to get better? Are you trying to *get out of God's will?*" Of course we can see how that position is ridiculous. Of course people who are sick want to get better. And God wants them to get better too. It is never His will for people to be sick. It is always His will to heal us. He always has been and always will be a healing God. He said, "I am the LORD who heals you" (Exod. 15:26). Jesus Himself bore your sicknesses (Matt. 8:17), and by His stripes you were healed, more than two thousand years ago (1 Pet. 2:24).

God doesn't cause sickness or any other trial and trouble. He is not the killer or destroyer. He is good!

Part of the confusion comes because people *do* learn lessons and gain insights from God when trouble or sickness comes. This happens, though, because when trouble or pain come, people run to God, press into His Word, listen to all their teaching CDs, and take lots of notes at church. If the sick person is confined to bed, he has plenty of time to seek God and listen to the Holy Spirit.

〜〜〜〜〜〜〜〜〜〜〜〜〜〜〜〜〜

God teaches you by His
Word and His Spirit, not by
trouble, trial, sickness, or any
other tool of the enemy.

〜〜〜〜〜〜〜〜〜〜〜〜〜〜〜〜〜

I think most people have been in this situation. You press into God because you're in trouble, and He answers. But of course, you *could* have learned the lesson at hand without being sick or in trouble. God doesn't need for you to be sick for Him to teach you something. Every time you press into God, He is there to meet you, teach you, and help you grow.

God teaches you by His Word and His Spirit, not by trouble, trial, sickness, or any other tool of the enemy.

You can avail yourself to His Word and His Spirit any time you want. In fact, it is advisable that you seek Him *before* trouble comes so you're ready to stand up strong and enforce your covenant.

Yes, there are tests and trials in life. Jesus Himself said, "In the world you will have tribulation" (John 16:33). He warned us! So we shouldn't be surprised when trouble comes. But we should be ready. Stay full of God's Word, and when trouble comes don't wring your hands and complain; instead take your authority in Christ. The good news is that there is more to that verse. Jesus finishes His sentence there by saying, "But be of good cheer, I have overcome the world."

Here's a way to keep track: if it's not good, it's not God! And that never changes.

God Answers Prayer

Another thing that never changes: God is still answering prayer. When we pray for big things and small things, He answers both requests. John 16:24 says, "Ask, and you will receive, that your joy may be full." Your heavenly Father *wants* you to ask! He wants to fill you with joy through answered prayer.

It amazes me how God cares about the big things *and* the small things in life. He has answered some sizable prayers for me. He has gotten me the job of my dreams, helped me buy and sell homes, healed the hearts of my sons and me, provided divine health for our bodies, met our needs, and blessed my sons with wonderful wives, just to name a few things. He constantly protects and guides us, and yet He is also aware of small details.

Not long ago God answered a simple prayer of mine in such a quick, remarkable way that I was reminded yet again about His character and how He never changes.

It happened when I was on a ministry trip to Europe. While I was gone, a friend stayed at my house to take care of my cat, water the lawn, and watch over the place. One day she accidently *slammed* into the storm door, which is all glass. She had been on the porch and turned to go back into the house. Apparently the glass door was so clean, she thought it was open and walked right into it.

Thankfully my friend wasn't hurt, and the glass didn't break. But the impact jammed the storm door frame into the molding, and it was stuck. I mean *stuck*. No amount of pushing, pulling, or kicking could get the door to open.

She told me about it when I got back, and I called a

handyman friend to come over to fix it. He was out of town for a while, so for the next couple weeks my front door was out of service. Everyone had to enter the house through the garage, which wasn't very handy.

One day I was having guests over, and I didn't want them to have to come in through the garage. Before they arrived, I decided to try one more time to kick the door open. But first I prayed a simple prayer, "Father, please help me get this door open." In my mind I figured that meant either I would somehow get it open by kicking it or that my handyman would call that day.

I put on my tennis shoes (for kicking power!), and from the inside of the house I kicked the doorframe as hard and mightily as I could. It came loose at the top but wouldn't budge on the bottom.

Next I went outside and tried pulling. Same result. Same discouragement. Just when I was about to give up, I heard a voice. "Don't you hate it when doors get stuck?" I turned to see a woman about my age and her dog coming up my driveway. I'd never met her before, but she introduced herself as a neighbor who lived down the street. I laughed and explained to her how the door had gotten stuck.

She offered to help: "How about if you go push from the inside, and I pull from the outside?" After some heavy-duty kicking and a little maneuvering with a screwdriver, we actually got the door open. Amazingly we didn't break or even bend it, and it opened and closed perfectly.

I had to marvel at the way God answered my simple prayer. A stranger just walked by and offered to help. Let's face it; these days most people would just walk on by if they saw a crazy lady kicking and pulling on her front door! In the grand scheme of the universe getting my front door unstuck wasn't that big of a deal. But it was important to me at that moment, and it was such a clear example to me that God still answers prayer. Nothing is too big or too small for Him, even a stuck door. He hasn't changed, and He has a million ways to get you the things you need.

Keep Believing

Maybe you've been believing for something for a long time and haven't seen an answer. My best advice is: don't stop now.

Anytime you hear someone say, "Well, I asked God for that, but He didn't answer," or, "I tried believing for that, but it didn't work," you're listening to someone who has *stopped believing* at some point. God's promise didn't change; the person did.

That is what happened in Matthew 14. You know the story. This is when Peter walked on water.

Not long after the miraculous feeding of five thousand people, Peter and the other disciples were on a boat when Jesus came along, walking on the water. The other disciples were freaked out (I have to admit that I would have been too), and they cried out, "It is a ghost!" (v. 26).

For reasons that defy comprehension, when Jesus said, "Be of good cheer. It is I: do not be afraid" (v. 27), Peter hollered, "Lord, if it is You, command me to come to You on the water" (v. 28). (Really? Is that first thing *you* would think of? Notice the other guys in the boat didn't say a word. I can't wait to talk with Peter about this when I get to heaven. What in the world possessed him to say that?)

You know what happened next. Jesus said, "Come" (v. 29), and based on that word from the Lord, Peter got out of the boat *and walked on the water*. He really did it! That is amazing! I've never seen anyone walk on water. Have you? Obviously Peter had more faith than anyone else on that boat. He believed the word of the Lord, and he walked on water.

Just as Peter took his first steps, trouble came. The wind began howling, and the waves were crashing. Peter took his eyes off Jesus and began to look at the tempest around him. In other words, he stopped holding fast to the word of the Lord ("Come"), and he looked at the rather daunting circumstances. As a result, he began to sink.

When Peter cried out to the Lord to save him, of course Jesus did. But Jesus didn't say, "Congratulations, Peter, you got out of the boat when no one else would, and you walked on water!" No, Jesus said, "O you of little faith, why did you doubt?" (v. 31).

The word *doubt* has the same root as the word *double*. To doubt is to be double-minded, or to believe two ways—first one way and then the other.[1] At first Peter believed the word of the Lord ("Come"), and faith rose up in his heart. Then he doubted.

In essence Jesus was saying, "Peter, why did you change? Why did you doubt? Why were you double-minded? You stopped believing Me and started believing the wind and waves."

When Jesus told Peter, "O you of little faith," I don't believe He was talking about the size of Peter's faith. It takes a big faith to walk on water. Rather, I believe Jesus was talking about the *duration* of Peter's faith. He had a *short burst* of faith.

Peter started out strong. He had big faith to get down out of that boat. He just couldn't sustain it long enough.

That happens to Christians today too. Some people have started out strong in their faith. But then something happens with their circumstances, and they stumble. They start believing what they *see* (or sometimes what they *don't* see), and they stop believing the Word of the Lord, the Bible.

So here's the deal. You need to keep your eyes on the Word. If Peter had kept his eyes on Jesus and ignored the wind and the waves, he would have made it safely to Jesus's side, and possibly even walked to shore with Him.

The wind and waves had nothing to do with walking on water. Think about it. Is water-walking possible? No. Even under the best conditions, if water is as smooth as glass, you can't walk on it—you need supernatural help.

Likewise it is going to take supernatural help for you to walk through this life or walk out of the valley of shadow. So what difference does it make if the waves are crashing and the wind is blowing?

Don't Become Discouraged

Not long ago I had a single friend who wants to get married say to me, "Everyone else seems to be getting married, and I'm not. I try not to be mad at them, but it's so unfair. I've been believing much longer than they have."

I felt compassion for her and her situation. Have you ever been praying for something, really desiring it with all your heart, and then someone else gets what you were believing for?

It's tempting to be jealous or discouraged when that happens. But let's be realistic here—does another person's answer to prayer take anything away from you? Is there a limited supply of God's blessings? The answer to both those questions is no. Someone else's prayer getting answered doesn't rob you of anything. If you're believing for a new car and your neighbor gets one just like the one you've prayed to get, that doesn't mean you won't get one too. That isn't the only car available.

In fact, you're in the same line as the person who got his prayer answered. You have the same God, who loves to bless and increase you. Instead of letting the other person's answer to prayer discourage you, rejoice with them. Romans 12:15 says, "Rejoice with those who rejoice." Rejoicing keeps you in position to receive.

There is no need to be jealous of someone else. Your heavenly Father hasn't taken His attention off you and switched it to the other person. If God answered someone else's prayer, it just means He's still in the prayer-answering business, so He will answer you too.

Now Engage

The circumstances in your life may change, but God's covenant with you will never change. His love and care for you are constant. Let these truths from God's Word build your confidence in His unchanging love and concern for you.

Front-Burner Truth: "In an ever-changing world, I know something that *never* changes."

I am the LORD, I change not.
—MALACHI 3:6, KJV

Jesus Christ is the same yesterday, today, and forever.
—HEBREWS 13:8

Even though things may have changed in my life, my covenant with God, bought by the blood of Christ, will *never* change. He will always love and care for me. I am standing on a solid foundation that is immovable.

> Whoever comes to Me, and hears My sayings and does them, I will show you whom he is like: He is like a man building a house, who dug deep and laid the foundation on the rock. And when the flood arose, the stream beat vehemently against that house, and could not shake it, for it was founded on the rock.
> —LUKE 6:47–48

My life is built firmly on the rock of Christ. I am established and grounded. Even when the storms of life come, my house and I will be left standing. I don't change or move just because of trouble or trauma.

> I will say of the LORD, "He is my refuge and my fortress; My God, in Him I will trust."
> —PSALM 91:2

Even in the midst of life's storms, this is God's Word to me, and it's more sure and lasting than the storms. My heavenly Father has promised to protect and hide me in times of trouble. He is my unchanging refuge and fortress when things are shifting and changing. I can count on that.

> The name of the LORD is a strong tower; the righteous run to it and are safe.
> —PROVERBS 18:10

I am the righteous, and the name of Jesus is my strong tower. There's no safer place to be! I run to this refuge that has been provided for me. I am safe.

> God is our refuge and strength, a very present help in trouble.
> —PSALM 46:1

My God is right here with me, especially when there's trouble. Every time I draw near to Him, He's always there. He is a very present help to me. That never changes.

> The thief does not come except to steal, and to kill, and to destroy. I have come that they may have life, and that they may have it more abundantly.
> —JOHN 10:10

The devil kills, steals, and destroys while Jesus came to give me abundant life. God is good, and the devil is bad. I won't get confused about that. If there is stealing or killing or destroying going on, it's the devil doing it, not God. They don't switch places or jobs. God is good and *only* good. Only good and perfect gifts come from Him.

> In the world you will have tribulation; but be of good cheer, I have overcome the world.
> —JOHN 16:33

I know there will be tests and trials in life because Jesus warned me about them, but He has overcome those troubles and given me His authority. God teaches me by His Word and His Spirit, not by trouble, trial, sickness, or any other tool of the enemy. I hide His Word in my heart *before* trouble comes, so I'm ready to stand strong and enforce the promises of God's covenant with me.

> Ask, and you will receive, that your joy may be full.
> —JOHN 16:24

God is still answering prayer—for big things and small things. He *wants* me to ask Him to meet my needs, and to fill me with joy through answered prayer. He always wants to get me jobs, heal me, provide for me, and bless me with wonderful relationships. He constantly protects and guides me, and He's fully aware of the small details of my life.

> O you of little faith, why did you doubt?
> —MATTHEW 14:31

I will keep my eyes on God's Word and not be moved by the wind and waves of life's circumstances. I won't change from believing to doubting. I won't be double-minded. I will keep believing!

Chapter Six

THERE'S A BLUEPRINT FOR YOUR LIFE

I F YOU ARE going to build a house, you can't start the process without a blueprint. The blueprint is the plan that a builder must have in order to build. It gives the builder a vision for what a house is supposed to look like. It also provides the guidelines for the workers who do the work with saws and nail guns.

Without a blueprint the house could turn out uneven. The construction crew wouldn't know what to do. Walls might not meet. Rooms might not be where they are supposed to be. Important elements such as plumbing, wiring, and doorways might be placed wrong. A hundred things could be wrong with the framing, and in the worst case scenario, the entire building could eventually collapse because it would be structurally unsound.

The Bible Is Your Guide

Here's another front-burner truth to keep your focus on: your blueprint for life is God's Word, the Bible. The Bible provides God's guidelines for you, the path for you to follow. Psalm 119:105 says the Bible is "a lamp to my feet and a light to my path." Right now you cannot see down the whole path for your life. The future is shrouded in darkness. But God's Word is a light to that darkness. It can show you the way to go. The Word gives you a vision for what your life is supposed to look like.

The Word teaches you how to walk through this life of a Christian, and it also shows you how to walk out God's specific plan for your life. Without it you could eventually collapse. The Bible is God talking to you. It is His Word to you, and His Word is His will.

> The Word gives you a vision for what
> your life is supposed to look like

I once talked with a young man who had camped in the land of hurt and questions. Several years earlier his best friend had died in a tragic accident. This young man simply couldn't get past the pain and loss.

By the time he came to see me, he was not sleeping, almost flunking out of school, and dabbling in drugs and alcohol. This young man was a born-again, Spirit-filled Christian. In fact, he'd been involved in church activities all of his life. Yet when he came to see me, he was struggling to make sense of a senseless accident.

After listening to him talk for quite a while, I asked, "How's your devotional life? Are you reading your Bible every day?" He was taken aback, and then answered sheepishly, "I haven't been reading it at all. I just stopped a while ago when I couldn't make sense of all this."

It was no wonder that the young man had gotten off track. He had stopped reading the instruction manual, the very source of help. There was nothing to shine a light into his darkness. He had lost the vision for his life just when he needed it most.

I challenged this young man to go back to reading the Word daily and see if it made a difference. I am happy to report that he did as I suggested, and it did make a difference. God's Word never fails. It is our blueprint for life.

Faith Comes by Hearing

It takes faith to walk out God's plan for your life—especially if something hard has happened and you have questions. And faith only comes from one place. Romans 10:17 says, "So then faith comes by hearing, and hearing by the word of God." If faith came another way, I would tell you. But it doesn't.

I've heard people say, "If I could just see a miracle, then I would have faith." If seeing miracles were enough in themselves, then the children of Israel would have had more faith than anyone, and they would have believed God about entering the Promised Land. The Book of Exodus records numerous miracles: water turns into blood, sticks transform into snakes, seas part. There are many miracles chronicled in the Old Testament and the New Testament, yet Hebrews 3:19 says, "We see that they could not enter in [to the Promised Land] because of unbelief."

Faith doesn't come from seeing miracles or hearing other people's testimonies; rather, it comes from hearing and believing the Word of God. The children of Israel didn't believe God's words; they believed more in the giants they could see. So they didn't get to enter into the Promised Land.

It is going to take faith for you to keep going through the valley of shadow. It is going to take faith to keep your questions on a back burner and move forward with God. First John 5:4 says, "This is the victory that has overcome the world—our faith." Your faith overcomes the trials and questions in your world. If you want to build up your faith, then turn to the Word of God, the blueprint.

Faith is simply believing what God has said more than what you see happening around you. It is believing something you can't see yet based on what God has promised in His Word. And it is your victory.

You were never meant to live on this planet without the Word of God. It is your lifeline. It is your instruction manual.

Colossians 3:16 says, "Let the word of Christ dwell in you *richly*" (emphasis added). Sadly many Christians allow the Word to dwell in them *poorly*. They read just a little bit. Every day you go without reading your Bible is a day you're trying to live life in your own strength. Believe me, that is too hard. The more you read, the better you live.

When my husband died, our associate pastor and his wife gave me a brand-new Amplified Bible as a gift to encourage me. I spent hours reading it. I had always been a Bible-reader, but at that time I spent every spare moment in it. I would run my finger down the pages like a five-year-old child learning to read. I *absorbed* it. I was *desperate* for it.

During that time period I fell more in love with Jesus

than ever, and eventually I came out of the valley of shadow. I was victorious. This all happened while I was reading my Bible.

> Every day you go without reading
> your Bible is a day you're trying
> to live life in your own strength.
> Believe me, that is too hard.

Psalm 119:92 says, "If your instructions hadn't sustained me with joy, I would have died in my misery" (NLT). That describes me. In the midst of my questions and fears, in the midst of leading a church by myself, and in the midst of raising two sons, I clung to God's Word, His instructions. I knew I had to. All of that time spent reading and meditating on the Bible settled me. It established my path. That is what it is meant to do. And it can do the same thing for you.

Proverbs 29:18 says, "Where there is no vision, the people perish" (KJV). The Word paints a picture of how God wants you to live. If you're not looking at the Word, you're liable to have the wrong picture, the wrong vision for your life. You're liable to get caught up in the hopelessness of this world and live a much lower life than God has provided for you.

The Bible isn't just another book. It is God's very being. You can't separate Him from His Word. His Word is His bond. Hebrews 4:12 says, "For the word of God is living and powerful, and sharper than any two-edged sword." This passage means that you definitely want to hide the Word of God in your heart so that you believe it more than you believe the temporary things going on all around you.

Read the Word

You can't know Jesus without knowing the Word. John 1:14 says, "And the Word became flesh and dwelt among us, and we beheld His glory, the glory as of the only begotten of the Father, full of grace and truth."

I've met some Christians who say, "I wish Jesus would talk to me." I tell them, "Read your Bible! That's Jesus, and He's talking to you." I've also heard people say, "I wish I knew God's will for my life." I tell them, "Read your Bible! His Word is His will."

I know that might sound too simple. You might be thinking, "There's got to be more to it than read your Bible, read your Bible, read your Bible." If there were, I would tell you. Instead I'm telling you that your answers are in the Word. Your faith gets built up when you read the Word. You can't expect to be an overcomer in this life without the Word of God in your heart, in your mind, and in your mouth.

Please understand, you don't read the Bible in order to earn and deserve God's blessings, saying, "I've read my three chapters today. I've been a good Christian. Now I've earned my blessings!" No. All the blessings already belong to you, in Christ. You didn't earn or deserve any of them. You received them by faith (Eph. 2:8–9). You get them by believing in the covenant that Jesus bought and paid for in His death, burial, and resurrection.

You read your Bible to remind yourself of those blessings.

You read the Word to feed and solidify your spirit and renew your mind to God's way of living (Rom. 12:2).

I've had people say to me, "I've read the Bible. It didn't work." To that I say, "Read it some more." Ask God to give you a desire for it. And keep reading.

> You can't expect to be an overcomer in this life without the Word of God in your heart, in your mind, and in your mouth.

I heard one minister say, "What you give yourself to, you create a desire for." I think that is true in every realm. Take golf for example. Years ago my husband's uncle taught him how to play golf. At first Brent didn't want to go to the golf course every day, but he kept going and kept playing. After a while he loved golf. He created the desire for the game by doing *more* of it, not doing less. It is the same with the Word—you can create a desire for it by spending *more* time reading it.

The Word of God is truth. Your circumstances are subject to change, but the Word is not. It has stayed the same and has never failed in thousands of years, and it is not going to fail now. *Read it some more.* Determine that you're going to keep your eyes on it, no matter how difficult your situation. Determine that you're going to believe it, no matter what else is happening all around you. Don't believe more in trouble than you do in the Word.

What does it mean to believe or stand on God's Word? It means that in the face of everything you encounter, you refuse to quit. You stand firm (Eph. 6:13–14). First Corinthians 15:58 says, "Therefore, my beloved brethren, *be steadfast, immovable,* always abounding in the work of the Lord, knowing that your labor is not in vain in the Lord" (emphasis added).

Don't believe more in trouble
than you do in the Word.

How do you remain steadfast? Instead of focusing on the negative aspects of a particular situation, decide to think about or meditate on God's Word. Choose to believe the promises it contains. Opt to hide the Word in your heart concerning your situation, and continue to speak what it says until there is a change.

Isaiah 55:11 says, "So shall My word be that goes forth from My mouth; it shall not return to Me void, but it shall accomplish what I please, and it shall prosper in the thing for which I sent it." God's Word never returns void. It *always* accomplishes what God has sent it forth to do.

If you quit, you won't gain anything. Keep putting your trust in God, even if you've suffered a loss, a surgery is pending, or the bank is calling. You have everything to gain because the promises in the Word are true, and they're yours to claim.

When trouble comes your way, it is not the time to let go of the Word or drop your faith. Keep believing! The only sure way to do that is to keep the Word flowing into your heart and mind. It is a simple truth. If you're not putting the Word into your heart and mind, you're inserting something else, possibly even a lie from the enemy. Nothing but the Word has the promise or power of God's truth. Jesus said, "If you abide in Me, and My words abide in you, you will ask what you desire, and it shall be done for you" (John 15:7). This is the way to have your prayers answered. Abide in Him by abiding in His Word.

Faith Is Like a Muscle

Friedrich Nietzsche once said, "That which does not kill us makes us stronger."[1] That is not a quote from the Bible, but it is a biblical principle. Every time you face a battle, your faith can get stronger.

Let me explain it this way: your faith is like a muscle. If you use it, it grows. If you don't use it, you still have it, but it is flabby and of little use, not able to push anything big out of your path.

One way you build the muscle in your body is to lift weights or to *push against* a firm object. I'm no expert, but as I understand it, when you lift weights, you're actually *tearing down* a muscle, and your amazing body works to repair and build it back up, bigger and better than before. That's why trainers tell you not to lift weights every day. You must allow time for the body to do the build-up repair.

Your faith works the same way. When trouble comes along and you push against it (resist the devil) by reading, meditating on, and speaking God's Word, your faith grows stronger and stronger, bigger and better than before. Note that you do not resist the devil by pushing against *him*; you resist the devil by pressing into the

Word so you can use the authority given to you by God to prevail.

Every time you face a battle,
your faith can get stronger.

This is why James 1:2 says, "My brethren, count it all joy when you fall into various trials." The trial isn't the joy, but the victory is. You can count your trials as joy because you're going to come out on the other side with the victory, and your faith can grow stronger in the process.

Don't misunderstand. Great faith doesn't come from great trials. Faith still only comes one way, from hearing and believing God's Word (Rom. 10:17). Many people go through great trials without their faith growing at all. It is the Word that builds your faith.

First Peter 1:6–7 says, "So be truly glad. There is wonderful joy ahead, even though you have to endure many trials for a little while. These trials will show that your faith is genuine. It is being tested as fire tests and purifies gold—though your faith is far more precious than mere gold. So when your faith remains strong through many trials, it will bring you much praise and glory and honor on the day when Jesus Christ is revealed to the whole world" (NLT).

Keep this truth in mind the next time trouble comes along. You can rub your hands together with glee and say, "Oh yeah, I've seen what God does in situations like this. My faith is getting stronger and stronger. I'm expecting the victory!"

Be a Doer of the Word

There is another aspect to building your faith and letting God's Word guide you. You need to do what the Bible says to do, not just read it. Scripture says, "But be doers of the word, and not hearers only, deceiving yourselves" (James 1:22).

Too often Christians read the Bible and even talk about it, but they don't live out what it says. In that case, it's not even the devil deceiving them—they deceive themselves.

To read the Word but not obey it is like buying a new lawn mower but never turning it on and mowing the lawn. You might show the mower to your neighbors and tell everyone you have it, but you're deceiving yourself if you think it is making your lawn look better while it is sitting in the shed. Until you get up off the couch, turn the mower on, and push it around your lawn, no grass is going to get cut.

Embrace the Power of Forgiveness

One thing we must *do,* according to the Word, is forgive. Forgiveness is a huge principle that cannot possibly be covered completely in this book, but I have to mention it because it is vital if you're going to move past your pain and questions to embrace your bright future.

I discovered how powerful forgiveness can be when I was counseling with a woman who had gone through a terrible childhood. She was abused both mentally and physically. As a result, her adult life was a mess. If you heard her whole story, you would understand why. I felt so bad for her.

After several meetings with this woman I was praying for her at home one night. I said, "Father, this is so unfair! It's not her fault she was born into this family that abused her. How can I help her? It can't be hopeless. You are the great equalizer. Is there an answer for her?"

I felt as if the Lord said, "Yes, there's an answer for her."

I replied, "I knew it! What's the answer for this precious sister?"

He said, "Forgiveness."

That stopped me short. It wasn't the answer I was expecting. I said, "No way! Are You sure, Lord? It doesn't seem like forgiveness will help her get over everything that's happened to her. It wasn't her fault."

The Lord told me something that I've never forgotten. He said, "Forgiveness is how My relationship started with you."

That is when I realized there was way more to the act of forgiving than I knew. This woman and I started studying forgiveness, and we found that it is God's way of starting over. It's how He started *you* over. He transformed you into a brand-new, born-again, righteous being by forgiving you. "And you, being dead in your trespasses and the uncircumcision of your flesh, He has made alive together with Him, having forgiven you all trespasses" (Col. 2:13).

When Jesus forgave you of your sins, you passed from spiritual death to spiritual life. Forgiveness is how God makes something new, how He starts things fresh. It is how He does do-overs.

The more this woman and I studied forgiveness, the more we learned that this is how God deals with mankind. He is not a grudge holder. He is a forgiving Father. Since we are His children, we should also forgive. Harboring unforgiveness is like drinking poison and expecting someone else to die.

Once this woman studied the Word, she had enough faith to forgive. When she actually forgave her family for the horrible things that had happened to her in her childhood, her life changed. She was able to receive God's love, which gave her the capacity to love people around her and mend relationships. It even affected her physical appearance. Her face looked lighter. The transformation was remarkable.

> Harboring unforgiveness is like drinking poison and expecting someone else to die.

As for me, I learned that forgiveness is the only way to cut the chains of a painful past and become free. Why drag the pain of horrible people or events into your future? Cut the chain and let go of the pain.

Have You Been Hurt?

Often when I talk with Christians about holding a grudge or harboring unforgiveness, they deny that they do it. After all, we know we're supposed to forgive, right? So let me ask the question another way. Have you been hurt? My guess is that if you've been alive longer than fifteen minutes, your answer is yes.

Everyone has been hurt at some point. But it is not OK to stay hurt. God doesn't want you to live with the pain. He wants you to live free of the hurts.

You might think, "But you don't know what they did to me!" That's true; I don't know. And I'm very sorry for the pain you've suffered. But my being sorry doesn't help you. It doesn't set you free.

It's not OK to stay hurt. God doesn't want you to live with the pain. He wants you to live free of the hurts.

Many times after I've taught on forgiveness, people approach me who want to explain how horribly they've been wronged, as if I might give them special permission to hold a grudge. But I never do it! I don't diminish what happened to them or say that it was OK. But I'm trying to help them get free, and that begins with forgiveness.

Sometimes when people have done you wrong, you want to tell everyone about it. You want them to agree that someone committed a horrendous act against you and you deserve to be mad. But agreement on how bad something was isn't going to help you get free! Rehashing it, telling others about it, and holding on to it just prolongs the agony. Forgiveness is the way to let it go once and for all.

I've met people who have tried to forgive but have struggled to do it. I know it can be hard. Sometimes the hurt goes so deep or the pain has been throbbing for a long time. But God just wants you to *want to* forgive. He'll help you do it! He'll do the work in your heart when you go to His Word and ask Him for the strength to forgive.

One time I was at a ladies' retreat in the mountains. For three straight days (nine services) I taught from the Word on forgiveness. There were only about thirty-five of us, so we met in a living room of one of the condos.

One woman sat in the back of the room for each meeting. She was so far back that no one could see her except me—and she cried *the whole time.* She didn't cry loudly, but for all nine services there were tears streaming down her face.

At the end of the last meeting we prayed together to forgive those who had hurt us. I had everyone write in their Bibles the date and whom they had forgiven. After a time of worship we all went to bed.

The next morning after breakfast, before we headed back to civilization, we had a short gathering, and some ladies gave testimonies about how God had moved in their lives during the retreat.

Toward the end of the testimony time the woman who had cried spoke up. She said, "Last night after we prayed and I forgave, I slept through the night *for the first time in twenty years.*" (Apparently unforgiveness can keep you awake at night!)

This woman told us that when she was a young girl, her family had joined a cult, and they had lived on a farming commune. She didn't go into detail about what happened, but the experience obviously had been traumatic for her. Later her parents divorced, and her family scattered. In her young mind her life was destroyed by this cult and in particular by the cult leader, whom she hated with a passion.

By the time this woman had come to the retreat, she had been a Christian for years, and many people had told her that she needed to forgive this cult leader. She had tried, but the hurt went too deep. She just couldn't forgive him in her own strength.

When we prayed, she was set free. Not only could she now sleep peacefully through the night, but she told us that she was also healed of a hearing loss.

It is one thing to hear that we should forgive. But it is a whole different thing to soak one's spirit in the Word until faith comes.

I believe that the only way this woman got to the point where she could finally forgive was by sitting for hours at that retreat, hearing God's Word. It gave her the faith she needed. The teaching reminded her of all that Jesus had forgiven in her life and painted a picture of what forgiving others looked like. She wasn't able to forgive until she had enough Word in her heart to make it happen.

> It is one thing to hear that we should forgive. But it is a whole different thing to soak one's spirit in the Word until faith comes.

Many Christians are similar to this woman. They know they should forgive. They wish they could or even have tried to do so, but the hurt goes too deep. The answer lies in letting God cleanse your heart with the water of His Word (Eph. 5:26). Jesus said we are clean because of the *Word* He's spoken to us (John 15:3). If you have a *lot* to forgive, you need a lot of Word. In a similar way, if you're facing a major sickness, you need a large amount of Word to believe for your healing.

You Can Forgive

This chapter is about the blueprint for our life—the Bible. God's Word is the only place to obtain a vision for a life of forgiveness (or healing or anything else). Just like this woman who cried her way through the retreat, we can't find the strength to forgive without the Word.

At the retreat the woman heard scripture after scripture that gave her faith to forgive. And then she decided to be a doer of what she had heard, not just a hearer. When she took the step of faith, she saw supernatural results.

You can too! You may have to forgive someone who treated you badly, did you wrong, or let you down. Maybe you have to forgive God, forgive a loved one, forgive someone for dying, or forgive yourself. The Word is the only way to get the power to forgive. Faith for forgiveness *will come.*

Here are some of the scriptures I talked about at that retreat. If you've had trouble forgiving or even if you haven't and just want to maintain a lifestyle of forgiveness, mark this page and spend time reading and meditating on these passages.

- Colossians 2:13
- Colossians 3:12–13

- Matthew 6:12–15

- Matthew 18:21–35

- Luke 6:35–37

- Luke 11:4

- Luke 23:34

- John 13:34–35

- 2 Corinthians 2:7–11

- Ephesians 4:30–32

- Romans 12:19–21

And whenever you stand praying, if you have anything against anyone, forgive him and let it drop
(leave it, let it go), in order that your Father Who
is in heaven may also forgive you your [own] fail-
ings and shortcomings and let them drop.
—MARK 11:25, AMP

I quoted the last one in its entirety because I love the
imagery of "Let it drop (leave it, let it go)." I can picture
you dropping a hurt, grudge, or aggravation into a pile
and walking away from it. Let it go! Don't ever go back
and pick it up again. Let God take care of it. Your part is
to cut the chain that's been binding you to the past and
walk away free.

Give Up the Reasons

Sometimes we humans think there are certain reasons
we can use to justify holding a grudge. Here are some
that I've heard.

"If I forgive the person who wronged me, he (or she) will get away with it."

Galatians 6:7 says, "Do not be deceived, God is not mocked; for whatever a man sows, that he will also reap." *The Message* renders this verse, "No one makes a fool of God. What a person plants, he will harvest." In other words, no matter what it looks like right now, the person who wronged you will not get away with it. He *will* reap what he has sown. But you leave justice to God. He's no fool. Meanwhile you forgive and get yourself free.

"If I forgive the person who wronged me, it's like saying what he (or she) did was OK."

Forgiveness is not condoning the wrong that was done. Forgiveness is only about getting free.

You're not accountable for
what others do, only for what
you do. Choose forgiveness
and walk away free.

"The person who wronged me doesn't deserve to be forgiven."

You didn't deserve forgiveness either, yet Jesus forgave your sins. Forgiveness doesn't have anything to do with deserving it. If everyone got what they deserved, everyone would die and go to hell. Don't throw the *d* word (*deserve*) around. You don't want to get what you deserve, and neither do I!

"The person who wronged me is not sorry."

Again, you forgive because God says to forgive and because forgiveness sets you free. It is how you cut the chains to the pain of the past. It is true; the person you're forgiving may *never* apologize or acknowledge the pain you suffered. Let it go anyway. You're not accountable for what others do, only for what you do. Choose forgiveness and walk away free.

"But someone has to pay!"

I'm here to tell you that Someone already has paid. Jesus paid for you and for me and for the person who hurt you. Even though revenge is a socially acceptable concept, it's *not* acceptable in God's book. Romans 12:19 says, "Dear friends, never take revenge. Leave that to the righteous anger of God. For the Scriptures say, 'I will take revenge; I will pay them back,' says the LORD" (NLT). Do you know why God says that? Because revenge is too hard on the human heart. Let Him handle it.

Whatever reasons you may have been using to hold on to unforgiveness, let them go. Give them up. Choose instead to be a doer of God's Word, and let Scripture help you move forward.

You *Can* Forgive

I once heard the story of a young woman whose father was brutally murdered. Two men were arrested for beating him to death. One was sentenced to life in prison with the possibility of parole; the other went to death row.

The young woman was full of hatred and bitterness toward the men who had killed her father. The man on death row died there. However, fourteen years later she actually met the man who had been sentenced to life in prison.

Meanwhile, God had been dealing with her, and she knew she had a choice to make. She decided to visit the man. When she went to visit him, she didn't know what she was going to say, but she planned at least to ask if he knew Jesus as his Savior. And as it turned out, during his time in prison the man had accepted the Lord, stopped using drugs, and joined a prison job-retraining program. He felt terrible about having killed someone and had prayed that the Lord would give him a chance to tell the family of his remorse.

"Forgiveness is unlocking the door to set someone free and realizing you were the prisoner."

As soon as the young woman met the man, he began telling her how sorry he was for what had happened. As he talked, the Holy Spirit prompted her to tell him she forgave him. And then something miraculous happened. As soon as she said the words, "I forgive you," she could see something lift off of him, as if a huge burden was gone.

Later she realized that the same thing had happened to her. When she released him from his terrible guilt, she was also released from all the anger and bitterness she'd been carrying around inside of her.

Sometimes forgiving is like doing physical therapy on a wounded limb. When you go to therapy and exercise that limb, it hurts. And sometimes because it hurts, you want to stop because you don't want to deal with the pain. But if you stop, the limb can't get better.

In the same way, if you draw back from forgiving, your own heart can't get better. As soon as you choose to release the hurt, let it go, and forgive, your heart can receive the healing and restoration it needs. I like what one minister says: "Forgiveness is unlocking the door to set someone free and realizing you were the prisoner."

If this young woman could forgive, you can forgive! Just like her, you can't change the past, *especially* if other people are involved. You can't control what other people do, but you *can* control your response. You can leave the hurts and anger of the past behind when you choose to follow the blueprint and forgive.

Now Engage

The Bible is your blueprint for life. Build your faith in God's power in your life by meditating on and declaring these truths from God's Word.

Front-Burner Truth: "I know the Bible is the blueprint for my life."

> Your word is a lamp to my feet and a light to my path.
> —Psalm 119:105

God's Word is the "blueprint" for my life. It provides me with His guidelines, the path for me to follow. It's a light to the darkness and shows me the way to go. It gives me a vision for what my life is supposed to look like. It teaches me how to walk this life of a Christian, and also how to walk out God's specific plan for me. It's

God talking to me—it's His will for me, the source of
my help.

> So then faith comes by hearing, and hearing by
> the word of God.
> —ROMANS 10:17

It takes faith to walk out God's plan for my life, and
faith comes from only one place: from hearing, believing,
and doing the Word of God. My faith overcomes the
trials and questions in my world, so I will build up my
faith daily by reading, studying, and meditating on the
Bible.

> Let the Word of Christ dwell in you *richly*.
> —COLOSSIANS 3:16,
> EMPHASIS ADDED

I won't let the Word dwell in me poorly or just a little.
I won't try to live life in my own strength. I will feed my
spirit on God's Word. I will read the Bible to renew my
mind to God's way of thinking. I'll keep reading it often
to create a greater desire for it.

> My brethren, count it all joy when you fall into
> various trials.
> —JAMES 1:2

When trouble comes along I will push against it (resist
the devil) with my faith. I count this situation as joy,
because I'm going to come out on the other side with
the victory, and because my faith can grow stronger in
the process. I can't wait to see how God will work it all
together for my good!

> And whenever you stand praying, if you have any-
> thing against anyone, forgive him and let it drop
> (leave it, let it go), in order that your Father Who
> is in heaven may also forgive you your [own] fail-
> ings and shortcomings and let them drop.
>
> —MARK 11:25, AMP

I will be a doer of God's Word and choose to forgive everyone who has hurt me, because I have been completely forgiven by God. I won't rehash the wrongs done against me or hold on to them. I'll leave them. I'll let them go. I'm free!

Chapter Seven

GOD IS STILL IN THE MULTIPLICATION BUSINESS

OFTEN WHEN YOU have gone through a trauma and have questions, you feel as though you have lost something, as if you are in some way diminished. It can seem as though something has been stolen from you or that you are on the decreasing side of life.

Sometimes you *did* lose something. When my husband died, I felt the loss very deeply—it was real. But I learned that the loss wasn't the end of the story. Even if it seems as if your life is *decreasing* and things are being taken *away*, don't be fooled. God is and always will be a God of increase.

Here is a front-burner truth that you want to meditate on: no matter what is happening right now, God is still in the multiplication business. He is working on an answer for you *right now.* God knows exactly how to get you from the land of loss to the land of increase.

God has provided increase for my sons and me, and He can do it for you too if you'll keep believing Him. He is faithful!

The Bible says, "The LORD shall increase you more and more, you and your children" (Ps. 115:14, KJV). Read that again! This promise is true for you and your family.

―――――――――――――――――――――――

God knows exactly how to
get you from the land of loss
to the land of increase.

―――――――――――――――――――――――

Another passage says, "Now he that ministereth seed to the sower both minister bread for your food, and multiply your seed sown, and increase the fruits of your righteousness" (2 Cor. 9:10, KJV).

Notice all of the great words in those verses: *increase, more,* and *multiply.* These passages reveal the very nature of your heavenly Father. And as you can see from the scriptures quoted above, He is the same in the old covenant and the new covenant. He doesn't do subtraction, only multiplication.

You can believe it! Spend less time thinking about what you've lost and focus on what you have and what He is going to bring into your life. God *is* working all things together for your good (Rom. 8:28). He knows exactly how to work everything out for you.

Here Is a Story of Multiplication

I have some wonderful friends, David and Marie, who obeyed the call of God on their lives. Once their kids were grown and out of the house, they moved to a reservation to minister to Native Americans.

God has greatly blessed David and Marie's work,

but their ministry hasn't grown without sacrifice, and increase didn't come overnight. They had to give up a lot, including their home. After several lean years it would have been easy for them to ask, "Why, God, why?" After all, they had forsaken all in order to obey Him.

The question may have come to their minds, but they did not give up. Neither did God. He had good plans in mind for them, just as He does for anyone who will believe and keep believing. In Mark 10:29–30 Jesus is quoted as saying, "Assuredly, I say to you, there is no one who has left house or brothers or sisters or father or mother or wife or children or lands, for My sake and the gospel's, who shall not receive a hundredfold now in this time."

I'll let Marie tell you the rest of the story in her own words:

> When we moved to the reservation, the housing prices were double what they had been in Boise. We felt that we would never be able to buy a home there unless God did something miraculous for us.
>
> For the first ten years we lived in a six-hundred-square-foot apartment. I was very content to be there, but from time to time I would remind the Lord of His promise in Mark 10:29–30 that in this lifetime He would give back homes to those who had given up homes for Him. Through a series of amazing circumstances, we closed on our current home only thirty days after we were prequalified! We got 100 percent financing, and it cost us only four hundred dollars to move in. The house even came full of furniture—beautiful stuff including

> dishes, silverware, pots and pans, a nice wool rug, and a table and chairs.
>
> We are on a mountaintop with an acre that is wooded with ninety-foot-tall pine trees. This is my dream home that God laid up for me!

This wonderful couple is faithful to God's call on their life. They gave up their lives in order to help others, and God knew just how to reward them. Hebrews 11:6 says, "But without faith it is impossible to please Him, for he who comes to God must believe that He is, and that He is a *rewarder* of those who diligently seek Him" (emphasis added).

Because your heavenly Father is a God of increase and a rewarder, He has a way of making your dreams come true in an even greater way than you expected.

Maybe you've experienced a loss or you're facing financial challenges today. Maybe all you can see is loneliness or loss or red ink and no sign of multiplication in your future. Let me remind you that God is your source, and He is a good one. He won't withhold any good thing from you (Ps. 84:11). When I pressed into His Word about provision and restoration, this truth went down into my heart, and in the years since my husband died, God has done more to prosper me and my children—in every way—than I ever could have imagined.

Don't look only to natural sources for your provision or to heal your heart. Keep your eyes on your God, who multiplies. Jesus said, "Beloved, I pray that you may prosper in all things and be in health, just as your soul prospers" (3 John 2). God wants you to prosper, and He knows just how to do it. The way to prosper your soul is to keep His Word before your eyes and believe it.

⌒⌒⌒⌒⌒⌒⌒⌒⌒⌒⌒⌒⌒⌒⌒⌒⌒⌒⌒⌒⌒⌒

Because your heavenly Father is
a God of increase and a rewarder,
He has a way of making your
dreams come true in an even
greater way than you expected.

⌒⌒⌒⌒⌒⌒⌒⌒⌒⌒⌒⌒⌒⌒⌒⌒⌒⌒⌒⌒⌒⌒

I like the way Paul talks about God who multiplies: "God can do anything, you know—far more than you could ever imagine or guess or request in your wildest dreams!" (Eph. 3:20, THE MESSAGE). That is the truth.

What About Job?

The story of Job is a perfect example of God multiplying someone after trouble hit. Much has been said about the Book of Job, and still many people don't understand it. The theme of Job's story is suffering, which most people don't necessarily want to talk about. In fact, at a glance Job can seem like a book about decrease instead of increase. But it is not!

There are lots of good things to say about Job. First, the Bible says, "[Job] was blameless and upright, and one who feared God and shunned evil" (Job 1:1). He had seven sons and three daughters, and his estate was substantial. Job 1:3 says, "This man was the greatest of all the people of the East."

Job had much, but one day everything collapsed. All that Job feared came upon him (Job 3:25), and everything he had was taken away from him. Marauding enemies stole his livestock and killed his servants, fire raged through his flocks and fields, all of his children died, he became deathly ill, and his wife turned on him.

Most of the Book of Job is about one man's personal suffering. But the suffering didn't last forever, and there was more to the story. Near the end of the book, Job 42:12 says, "Now the LORD blessed the latter days of Job more than his beginning." The passage goes on to list all the belongings and family that were restored to him. Job's story ends well too: "Job died old, and full of days" (v. 17).

God is a restorer! He multiplies. You may feel as if you have lost some things. Obviously Job felt that way. But he didn't quit on God. He didn't have nearly as good a covenant as you have in the blood of Jesus, but he refused to turn his back on God. Despite everything bad that happened to him, he said, "Though He slay me, yet will I trust Him" (Job 13:15).

You Should Not Limit God

If you get into a *decrease* or *loss* mentality when you have questions, it is tempting to settle for less than God's best.

Don't do it! With your questions simmering along on a back burner, keep reminding yourself of who your heavenly Father is. He is a God of increase, a God who multiplies. The devil may have stolen something from you, but God knows how to make it up to you!

First John 4:4 says, "You are of God, little children, and have overcome them, because He who is in you is greater than he who is in the world." God your multiplier is greater than anything the devil has ever done.

Don't limit the greatness of God's power toward you (Eph. 1:19), and don't settle for less than His best.

I once heard a story about some college students who settled for less. On the day of their literature final their professor stood before the class and offered them a choice. He said, "If you want a guaranteed automatic C, you can leave right now and not take the test." Half the class left, delighted that they would pass the class without having to take the test.

> The devil may have stolen
> something from you, but God
> knows how to make it up to you!

To the remaining students who stayed behind, the professor spoke about ten minutes, sharing some things from his heart. He told them that he was proud of them for aiming higher than a C, and that good things come to those who are willing to work hard, maintain their character, and help others. He also told them to expect good things and to keep demanding more of themselves than mediocre.

Then he said, "For those of you who stayed behind and were willing to try for better than a C on the test, I'm giving you an automatic A. You're dismissed."

I imagine that when the first group of students heard what had happened, they were kicking themselves. They had been willing to settle for a C. To be safe, they had limited their potential, and they missed out on a greater opportunity.

Have you ever limited God by settling for mediocre

because it sounded easier or you weren't willing to expect more? I must admit that I have done this a time or two. I have played it safe and settled for "good enough" when "awesome" was just around the corner. There have been times when I should have expected more or put in a little more effort. I don't want to ever fall into that trap again. I never want to limit God.

James 4:2 says, "You do not have because you do not ask." I think you should ask for everything that God has promised to give. You should expect everything that would benefit you and those you are called to help. God's Word clearly shows that He wants to lavish His blessings on you. Don't settle for anything less. Don't minimize the possibilities just because you have questions or feel pain.

Get Your Hopes Up

I've met many people who, either by their words or their actions, say, "Don't get your hopes up." The logic behind that, I suppose, is that if you don't get your hopes up, then you won't be disappointed.

That is a terrible way to live. Hope can be defined as "to desire with expectation of obtainment" and "to expect with confidence: trust."[1] That sounds like a better way to live than dialing back your expectations to nothing just to protect yourself.

I think God wants us to lift up our eyes and hearts, and then begin to believe the best. I say get your hopes up as high as you can. Start using your God-given imagination to embrace all the possibilities He has for you. Romans 15:13 says, "Now may the God of hope fill you with all joy and peace in believing, that you may abound in hope by the power of the Holy Spirit."

A heart full of hope brings you joy and peace in believing and extends the power of the Holy Spirit toward you so that you, in turn, can extend it to others. You should crank your hope in God all the way up! His plans are bigger than anything you can think up. After all, He is the God of increase.

You and I aren't the same as we were before we knew God. At that time we were "without Christ, being aliens...and strangers from the covenants of promise, having no hope and without God in the world" (Eph. 2:12). That is not who we are now. Redeemed by Jesus, we have become God's children, and we should act like it. We should *hope* like it.

> His plans are bigger than anything you can think up. After all, He is the God of increase.

What a terrible thing it is to have no hope. How sad that so many people are in that condition today. Christians who have hope should have great compassion on people who have little or no hope. And we should desire to tell lost people about Jesus.

In addition to prompting compassion to rise up in you, I hope that seeing people who have little or no hope makes you realize that you are different—you have hope. You have Christ! You aren't living life on this planet as a hopeless person.

As you move forward, keep your hope dialed up to

high. Always expect God's supernatural intervention in your life. As children of Almighty God you aren't limited to a natural way of living, so don't settle for anything less than the best.

Recognize the Seasons of Life

In life there can be times of multiplication, but there can also be times of drought and hardship. Have you ever noticed how these seasons of life mirror the passing of the natural seasons of winter, spring, summer, and fall? Ecclesiastes 3:1 says, "To everything there is a season, a time for every purpose under heaven."

Different things happen in different seasons, both naturally and spiritually. Naturally speaking, in the winter it is cold and barren. Nothing blooms. Animals hibernate. When spring comes, it is a time of freshness and new life. During the summer there is heat. In the fall it is time for the harvest.

Just as there are seasons in nature, our lives have seasons. Some are barren and cold. Some are filled with new hope and new life. In some seasons we plant. And we water. And we don't see anything come up for a while. But then comes the harvest season.

If you're in a winter season right now, don't quit or get discouraged. Spring is coming in your life, just as surely as it comes in the natural realm every year. God hasn't stopped multiplying you. Your season of increase is coming if you'll simply keep believing.

The cold barrenness of winter or the scorching heat of summer is only temporary. The tests and trials of the hard seasons don't change your destiny. During the winter and summer times of your life seeds are growing under the ground.

When my children were babies, I can remember thinking, "I can't wait until they walk." And when they did, it added new challenges to my life—for one, they no longer stayed where I put them.

> God hasn't stopped multiplying you.
> Your season of increase is coming
> if you'll simply keep believing.

Then I thought, "I can't wait until they go to school." Soon enough they did! And again there was a whole new set of challenges, for them *and* for me. After a while I realized there was always going to be a new season. I might as well not get in a hurry, but rather enjoy the season we were in, and then embrace the next one when it comes.

There are always going to be seasons in your life. If you don't like the season you're in right now, there's good news: it's going to change. Conversely if you love the season you're in, be sure to enjoy every moment because it too is going to change.

If you're in a season of multiplication right now, enjoy it. And save up! If you're in a season of barrenness or heat, don't worry—your season of increase is coming. Yes, God is still in the multiplication business. Keep that truth on your front burner!

Now Engage

God knows how to get you from the land of loss to the land of increase. To build your faith that increase *is* coming, meditate on and declare these truths from God's Word.

Front-Burner Truth: "I know God is still in the multiplication business."

> The LORD shall increase you more and more, you and your children.
> —PSALM 115:14, KJV

No matter what's going on right now, I know that my God is increasing me. He's working on something for me right now. This story isn't over. God knows exactly how to get me from the land of loss to the land of increase.

> Beloved, I pray that you may prosper in all things and be in health, just as your soul prospers.
> —3 JOHN 2

God is my source, and He's a good one. He is prospering me as I prosper my soul by keeping His Word before my eyes. He wants me to prosper! And He can do anything—more than I could ever imagine or guess in my wildest dreams.

> Now the LORD blessed the latter days of Job more than his beginning.
> —JOB 42:12

When the devil stole from Job, God restored every-thing back to him and even more. He can do the same for me! God is a restorer and a multiplier in my life. I won't quit on God. I'll stay in faith. It's turning out very, very well for me, in Jesus's name.

> You are of God, little children, and have overcome them, because He who is in you is greater than he who is in the world.
> —1 JOHN 4:4

The devil may have stolen from me, but God knows how to make it up to me. He is greater than what the devil has done. I will not limit the greatness of God's power toward me, and I won't settle for less than His best.

> Now may the God of hope fill you with all joy and peace in believing, that you may abound in hope by the power of the Holy Spirit.
> —ROMANS 15:13

I'm going to keep my hopes up! I refuse to dial back my expectations just to protect myself from disappoint-ment. I believe for the best. I'll use my God-given imag-ination to embrace all the possibilities He has for me, because His plans are bigger than any I can think of. He is the God of increase.

> To everything there is a season, a time for every purpose under heaven.
> —ECCLESIASTES 3:1

I understand that life has seasons—some are barren and cold, some are filled with new hope and new life. No matter what season I'm in right now, I won't quit or get discouraged. God hasn't stopped multiplying my seed sown. I will enjoy each season of my life and embrace the next one when it comes. In every season God is still in the multiplication business.

Chapter Eight

YOU HAVEN'T
LOST YOUR PLACE

HERE IS ANOTHER front-burner truth: even if you have questions, God hasn't fallen off the throne—and you haven't fallen either.

The Bible says that if you have received Jesus as your Savior, then you are seated with Him in heavenly places. "Even when we were dead in trespasses, [God] made us alive together with Christ (by grace you have been saved), and raised us up together, and made us sit together in the heavenly places in Christ Jesus" (Eph. 2:5–6).

The moment you said yes to Jesus, you were made alive and raised up to sit with Him. Notice, it was God who seated you there. You didn't seat yourself. Therefore, your heavenly position hasn't changed just because something happened (or didn't happen) to you on earth. You're still seated with Jesus. You haven't lost your place.

The View From Up There

What does the view look like from where you're sitting with Jesus at the right hand of the Father? Ephesians says that you're "far above all principality and power and might and dominion, and every name that is named, not only in this age but also in that which is to come" (Eph. 1:21).

This passage of Scripture goes on to say that God "put all things under His feet, and gave Him to be head over all things to the church, which is His body, the fullness of Him who fills all in all" (Eph. 1:22–23). If the devil is under Jesus's feet, he's under your feet too.

What does your position in Christ mean to you? For one thing, it means you're looking *down* on your problems and fears. Everything that the enemy does is *under* your feet.

Have you ever flown in a plane and looked down from about ten thousand feet? If it's a clear day and you can see all the way to the ground, you can spot vehicles on the freeways and houses on tree-lined streets. Everything looks very small from ten thousand feet in the air. You have a bird's-eye view, and everything looks peaceful and in order.

> If the devil is under Jesus's
> feet, he's under your feet too.

From that distance you can't see the weeds in the front yards or the paint chipping off the houses. You can't see the dents in the cars or bugs crawling around on the ground. You can't see any of the myriad little things that can make life unpleasant. At that distance imperfections and irritants disappear.

Likewise from your place in heavenly places, seated

next to God with Jesus, your troubles and fears look small too! It is important to remember where you're seated and that you have the same viewpoint of problems and imperfections that Jesus does. They should seem small to you in the big picture of your life in Christ.

The Bible tells you to magnify the Lord (Ps. 34:3). Often people magnify their problems instead. What happens when you magnify something? It gets bigger. Don't spend all your time focusing on and magnifying the troubles or fears in your life. When you do that, they just get bigger.

Instead, enjoy your place in Christ, seated at the right hand of your Father. Think about being seated there. Think about the blessing and authority the position gives you, and what a safe place it is. Magnify the Lord, not your troubles or fears. Be sure to look at life from your position in Christ. You may feel low down, but in reality you are up high in heavenly places with Him.

You Have an Inheritance

No matter what happens in your life, you haven't lost your place in Christ, and therefore you haven't lost your inheritance either. Ephesians 1:11 says, "In Him also we have obtained an inheritance." Galatians 3:29 says, "And if you are Christ's, then you are Abraham's seed, and heirs according to the promise." If you have received Jesus as your Savior, then you are His heir and you have an inheritance.

If your grandfather passed away and left you an inheritance, not long after his death there might be a reading of his most recent will and testament. This legal document would declare your grandfather's wishes for the disbursing of his estate, specifically naming the recipients of his possessions, rights, and obligations. It is a way for him to speak from beyond the grave and say, "It's my will for you to have this."

If you have received Jesus as
your Savior, then you are His heir
and you have an inheritance.

Of course, an inheritance comes *after* someone has died, not before. Hebrews 9:16 says, "For where there is a testament, there must also of necessity be the death of the testator."

This is exactly what happened when Jesus died, except that His will and (new) testament are available to anyone who will receive Him and become a member of the family (John 3:16). His will, which leaves an inheritance to you, is more binding in the kingdom of heaven than your grandfather's will is here on earth. There is no contesting God's will and testament. It is settled forever in heaven (Ps. 119:89).

Your grandfather might have named your cousin in his will and given him part of the inheritance. Most relatives would be glad to be included, but what if your cousin said, "I don't believe it! I have questions." Or what if he said, "I never liked grandfather, and I don't want any part of his inheritance."

Would your cousin's protests change the will? Not one bit. The receiving of the inheritance would be up to your cousin. He could walk away from it if he wanted to, but that would not change your grandfather's directions.

The Testament has been written. God's will has been clearly outlined, and it contains all the things He has given us as the result of Jesus's death. But some people simply won't believe it. Some don't even read it. Many just walk away.

The good news is the will hasn't changed because of your circumstances, and it never will. The inheritance is still available for anyone who will step up and say, "Yes, that's mine."

I want to be one of those Christians who believe God's promises and step up to receive them, don't you? The truth is that Jesus is Lord, and you are seated with Him. Your inheritance is completely intact. It belongs to you! No one can take it away.

Moreover, your inheritance is more than enough to provide for your needs, protect you, and help you fulfill God's plan in the earth. Ephesians 1:3 says, "Blessed be the God and Father of our Lord Jesus Christ, who has blessed us with *every spiritual blessing* in the heavenly places in Christ" (emphasis added). You have everything you need to live a life of victory.

Jesus has given us authority to go into all the world and represent Him to those who don't know Him. You have a place and a calling, and your inheritance is intact.

You Are Part of a Body

Just as your inheritance is still in place, so is your place in the body of Christ. You haven't lost your place just because of something that's happened. The entire chapter of 1 Corinthians 12 talks about how the body of Christ is made up of many parts, and as a believer you are one of them. Verse 12 says, "For as the body is one and has many members, but all the members of that one body, being many, are one body, so also is Christ."

You were never meant to be alone. Humans are herd animals, designed to travel in packs. When you asked Jesus to be your Savior, you joined His family, which is called the body of Christ. Hebrews 10:24–25 says, "Let us consider one another in order to stir up love and good works, not forsaking the assembling of ourselves together, as is the manner of some, but exhorting one another, and so much the more as you see the Day approaching." We need each other! We need to gather together. That is why God has established and ordained the local church.

> The inheritance is still available
> for anyone who will step up
> and say, "Yes, that's mine."

Ephesians 4:16 explains how each of us has a "supply," an anointing, a way of being that benefits and knits together the whole body. First Corinthians 12 says that each part of the body is important, even the weaker parts.

I've known people who have used hurtful circumstances or tough questions as a reason to separate themselves from the body. Sometimes they become mad because another Christian (even a minister) has caused an offense, acted like a hypocrite, behaved badly, or been a taker instead of a giver. As a result, they may stop coming to church.

Running away from church and other believers is the

worst thing you can do. For one thing, it is God who places you in the body. First Corinthians 12:18 says, "But now God has set the members, each one of them, in the body just as He pleased." He has placed you where it pleases Him, even if that place isn't always comfortable. There are no perfect churches. After all, people are there. It is important to remember to stay in your place to please God, not to please yourself.

It is important to understand that separating from the body, from your herd, makes you highly vulnerable to the devil. For example, becoming mad at a pastor is a common problem that causes people to fall right into Satan's trap. If the enemy can create strife between your Word-bringer (pastor) and you, he has you right where he wants you. First Peter 5:8 says, "Be sober, be vigilant; because your adversary the devil walks about like a roaring lion, seeking whom he may devour." Notice it doesn't say he *will* devour you; rather, it says that he *may* devour you. This is an important distinction. Satan only has the power to devour when you give it to him. Remember that he is a defeated foe, and you have authority over him. So don't give him permission.

Satan is looking for someone whom he *may* devour. Often that is someone who is out of position, separated from the rest of the body. Often it is the person who is harboring an offense or hurt.

Think about a hungry lion in the wild, prowling in the tall grass behind a herd of antelope. What is that lion looking for? He's looking for a lone antelope, one that has wandered off from the group. A lion rarely attacks an entire herd, but instead will pounce on the one off to the side, because it has left the safety of the group and is easier to pick off. Don't let trouble or questions separate you from the body where God has placed you.

You need to stay with your herd. It is where you're safest. There is power in numbers, power in hearing the Word from a pastor every week, and power in accountability. Whether you agree with everything your pastor says, you still need a shepherd, especially if you're hurt or have questions. The church is where your help is.

> Don't let trouble or questions separate you from the body where God has placed you.

Hebrews 13:17 tells us, "Obey your spiritual leaders, and do what they say. Their work is to watch over your souls, and they are accountable to God. Give them reason to do this with joy and not with sorrow. That would certainly not be for your benefit" (NLT). Unless God tells you otherwise, stick with the pastor who's watching after your soul, and make sure you do it with joy. This can only happen if you stay in your place.

Being part of a body is not just about safety and accountability. The body needs you—your gift and your supply. You are happiest when you're using the gift God has given to you to bless others. Being part of a body also helps to keep your mind on God's concerns, specifically building His church. And it keeps your mind off your troubles. When you're a part of a body and using your gifts, something bigger than you is going on.

Jesus Knows When
Your Heart Has Been Broken

Jesus said, "The Spirit of the LORD is upon Me, because He has anointed Me....He has sent Me to heal the brokenhearted" (Luke 4:18). Jesus knows about your pain, and He knows exactly how to heal your broken heart. He is the only one who can fix it.

Often I meet people who have had their hearts broken or suffered some terrible event, and in the midst of their questions they are also gun shy. By gun shy I mean that their heartbreak makes them guarded. They fear entering into or maintaining relationships. They will not reach out to people. And they refuse to move toward their dreams. They live in fear, behind walls they've erected to protect themselves.

When I see this happening in people's lives, it makes me so sad for them. A horrible event ends up defining them, instead of letting God's grace and His plan define the next chapters of their life.

I want to encourage you to *not* back away from life just because you are heartbroken, hurt, or disappointed. I know the pain is real, and it *will* probably take some time to heal.

But when we know who we are in Christ and we remember where we're seated, we can be brave. We can forgive, move on, and be willing to enter into life's stream again. And we can do it with confidence, knowing that Jesus is available to help us through any future situation because we haven't lost our place.

I once met with a young woman who had been divorced for a couple of years. She wanted to talk with me because she was finding herself attracted to another man. This was difficult because her husband had left her for another woman, and she had suffered rejection because of it. Understandably she was hesitant to love again.

> Jesus know about your pain,
> and He knows exactly how
> to heal your broken heart.

After all she'd been through, she was afraid of her feelings. She wasn't sure she trusted herself anymore. Her thought was if she could be trusted in the first place, then she wouldn't have picked the wrong guy to marry the first time.

As she and I talked, I helped her to see that there is no reason to let a past failure determine how to live the rest of life. Yes, she needed to examine herself and maybe sharpen her relationship tools—she should learn everything she could from the things that had happened to her and make necessary adjustments—but she shouldn't let the heartbreaking past define her or rob her of a bright future. That would be living a life of fear, and that is what Jesus came to deliver people from.

First John 4:18 says, "There is no fear in love; but perfect love casts out fear." When you know that you are perfectly loved by God and seated with Him in heavenly places, it gives you the boldness to try again. You can be brave because you have a safety net.

It comes down to knowing who you are in Christ, knowing you haven't lost your place, and knowing that even if you take a chance and get your heart broken again, He will be there to heal you and lift you up.

Live to the fullest! Don't back off from people or situations unless God tells you to. As the saying goes, no guts, no glory—no risk, no reward. Don't run away or refuse to engage. Be brave! Don't be afraid to interact and try new things.

You can't live an insulated life. It is not good for you or for the people around you who need you to engage in their lives. Even if you try and fail again, Jesus will still be the healer of the brokenhearted tomorrow!

You Can Dream Another Dream

At some point in life everyone has lost a dream. When that happens, you have to make a choice. You can either set up a camp in the land of disappointment and regret or get up and dream another dream. When you know your place in Christ, you have the supernatural strength and determination to keep going.

Christian author and motivational speaker John C. Maxwell once said, "Dreams don't work unless you do."[1] To me that means that every day you need to throw back the covers, get out of bed, put one foot in front of the other, and move on with life. It takes effort to dream another dream, but you can do it!

The phrases "don't be afraid" and "fear not" appear in the Bible at least 150 times and perhaps as many as 365 times, depending upon the translation. I haven't counted them, so I don't know the total for sure, but you get the point. The Bible repeatedly says, "Don't be afraid!" That is because *God doesn't want you to be afraid.* This means that you don't have to be afraid of people, failure, or loss.

Be willing to try again. Get back on that horse and ride. Your safety net is in place. You haven't lost your place in Christ. All His power and love are still backing you—all the resources of heaven are still available to you!

Be brave! Don't be afraid to
interact and try new things.

So make it a matter of prayer and be willing to dive in when the Holy Spirit leads you. Because of your position in Christ you are a victory going somewhere to happen. Jesus is still firmly on the throne, and you are still firmly seated there with Him in heavenly places.

Your Place of Rest and Peace

There are many benefits to being seated in your place next to Christ in heavenly places. One benefit is that it is a peaceful, restful place.

From your place at the right hand of the Father you can gauge your life by peace. Colossians 3:15 says, "Let the peace of God rule in your hearts." I like the way the Amplified Bible says it: "And let the peace (soul harmony which comes) from Christ rule (act as umpire continually) in your hearts [deciding and settling with finality all questions that arise in your minds...]."

Let God's peace act as your umpire. What does an umpire do? In baseball he is the one running the game. He is the person who decides which player is safe and which one is out. He is in charge, and if there is a dispute among the players or coaches, he has the final say-so.

Let peace be in charge of your life. When deciding what to think on, make peace the priority. When making a decision, check your heart and make sure it is at peace. Let peace have the final say-so in every aspect of your life.

The old hymn "Constantly Abiding" opens with the line, "There is a peace in my heart that the world never gave, a peace it cannot take away."[2] The peace the songwriter is talking about doesn't come from circumstances or surroundings. It comes from the inside, where the Holy Spirit abides. It comes from God.

In John 14:27 Jesus promised to leave us His supernatural peace: "Peace I leave with you, My peace I give to you; not as the world gives do I give to you. Let not your heart be troubled, neither let it be afraid." Read that again! This is the peace you want as a guide for your life.

Sometimes when I think of peace, I picture myself somewhere outdoors, perhaps reclining in a lounge chair beside a beautiful mountain lake. A gentle breeze wafts by as I sip a cool drink. Now that is peaceful. But that is not the peace Jesus left for His followers. His peace isn't on the outside; it is on the inside! You can know His peace at any time and in any place, even when stuck in a traffic jam at 5:00 p.m. when it is 105 degrees outside, your car overheats, and your kids are screaming in the backseat. *That's* when you need supernatural peace! And that's the peace you can call upon from your position in heavenly places.

How in the world can you live in that peace? You have to keep your eyes on Jesus and on His Word. Ephesians 1:11–12 says, "It's in Christ that we find out who we are and what we are living for. Long before we first heard of Christ and got our hopes up, he had his eye on us, had designs on us for glorious living, part of the overall purpose he is working out in everything and everyone" (THE MESSAGE).

> Let peace have the final say-so
> in every aspect of your life.

As you remind yourself daily who you are and where you are seated in Him, you can live out that glorious life He designed for you. It takes effort to keep your peace, but it is worth it. Don't give it up. Do whatever it takes to maintain your place in Christ and your place of peace.

Now Engage

God hasn't fallen off the throne, and you haven't lost your place. To help maintain your peace and your place in Christ, meditate on and declare these truths from God's Word.

Front-Burner Truth: "I know I haven't lost my place."

> Even when we were dead in trespasses, [God] made us alive together with Christ (by grace you have been saved), and raised us up together, and made us sit together in the heavenly places in Christ Jesus.
>
> —EPHESIANS 2:5–6

I am seated with Christ in heavenly places! Even though I have questions, God hasn't fallen off the throne—and

I haven't fallen either. It was God Himself who seated me there, and that position in Him hasn't changed just because something happened. I haven't lost my place.

> ...far above all principality and power and might and dominion, and every name that is named, not only in this age but also in that which is to come. And He put all things under His feet, and gave Him to be head over all things to the church, which is His body, the fullness of Him who fills all in all.
> —EPHESIANS 1:21–23

Since the devil is under Jesus's feet, he is under my feet too. I'm looking *down* on my problems and fears. From my viewpoint my troubles and fears look small in the big picture of my life in Christ. I will magnify the Lord, enjoying my place at His right hand with all its blessings and authority.

> In Him also we have obtained an inheritance.
> —EPHESIANS 1:11

I am an heir of Jesus—I inherited everything of His when He died. The will hasn't changed because of my circumstances, and it never will. My inheritance is completely intact, and it is more than enough.

> For as the body is one and has many members, but all the members of that one body, being many, are one body, so also is Christ.
> —1 CORINTHIANS 12:12

I am part of the body of Christ. Removing myself from other Christians would make me vulnerable to the devil and would leave the body without my supply. So I won't separate myself unless God says so. I'll stick with my herd and my spiritual leaders. I'll stay in my place.

> The Spirit of the LORD is upon Me, because He has anointed Me....He has sent Me to heal the brokenhearted.
> —LUKE 4:18

Jesus is the healer of my broken heart—both now and in the future. I trust Him. I won't back away from life out of fear of getting hurt again. I won't live behind emotional walls or let past failure determine my future. I'll learn from what has happened, then I'll forgive, move on, and be willing to live and love to the fullest.

> And let the peace (soul harmony which comes) from Christ rule (act as umpire continually) in your hearts [deciding and settling with finality all questions that arise in your minds].
> —COLOSSIANS 3:15, AMP

I will let peace be in charge of my life. When I'm deciding what to think on, I'll make peace the priority. When making a decision, I'll check my heart and make sure it's at peace. I'll let peace have the final say-so in every aspect of my life. Jesus left me His supernatural peace, and I will let it guide my life.

Chapter Nine

YOU ARE LOVED

Here is another front-burner truth you can focus on: no matter what has (or hasn't) happened in your life or how many questions you have about it, you are still perfectly loved by the Most High God. His love for you will never fail; it will never stop. The Bible says, "Love never fails [never fades out or becomes obsolete or comes to an end]" (1 Cor. 13:8, AMP).

Nothing can separate you from this love God has for you. The apostle Paul said it this way: "For I am persuaded that neither death nor life, nor angels nor principalities nor powers, nor things present nor things to come, nor height nor depth, nor any other created thing, shall be able to separate us from the love of God which is in Christ Jesus our Lord" (Rom. 8:38–39).

No human has ever loved you like this! God's love never quits or fades out because of something you did or didn't do. It doesn't stop because something happened or hasn't happened. You *cannot* be separated from your heavenly Father's love.

This isn't natural human love or the Hollywood movie kind of ooey, gooey love. This is not a feeling; it is a spiritual force. This is called "agape love," the love of God. Agape love is unconditional. It is at the core of God's nature. It is a love that does what is best for you at every turn, whether that means correcting you (Heb. 12:6) or bestowing every blessing on you (Eph. 1:3).

Yes, God will sometimes correct you, much as a loving parent must correct a child who needs it. If I'm doing something the wrong way—like a math problem, a situation on the job, or in a relationship—I want to get it corrected so I won't continue doing it wrong! God doesn't correct us cruelly—He doesn't put a trial on us to "teach us something." He corrects us by His Word and by His Spirit. He is our Heavenly Father—anything He does in your life, even correction, He does because He loves you.

This love comes from the heart of God. It is not based on your goodness; rather, it is based on *His* goodness.

There Is Always More

No matter how much you know that God loves you, there is always more to know. You will never plumb the depths of His love for you.

> This love comes from the heart of God. It is not based on your goodness; rather, it is based on *His* goodness.

At the time of my husband's death, I was a Christian. I loved God. I was a Word girl—I believed and practiced faith in God's Word. I preached the gospel. But it wasn't until after Brent died and I pressed into God like never before that I fell completely in love with God. The more time I spent with Him, the more I loved Him. And I began to understand that He has this kind of love for all of His children.

Each believer is at a different level of understanding His love. You might feel completely loved by Him, and that is good. But He loves you even more!

On the other hand you might not be at all sure of God's love. Everywhere I go, I meet Christians who aren't sure. They know that God is love, but they don't know how He feels about *them personally.*

Maybe you are uncertain about God's love. Maybe you weren't well-loved growing up. Maybe people have told you, "I love you," and then betrayed you. Maybe you've been treated badly, and instead of understanding love, your life has been based on suspicion and pain. I understand. But that is not how God wants you to live.

One time when I was preaching a message about how much God loves us, a woman came up to me after the service. She told me that she had a PhD in religion and knew a lot about God and the Bible, but she had never fully believed the concept that God actually loved her. She said, "I've never really grasped the 'love thing.'"

I wanted to cry out, "But that is *the* thing! It is what the whole gospel is based on!"

How can you be a bearer of the message of God's love if you aren't sure of it yourself? How can you "walk in love," as the Bible instructs (Eph. 5:2), when you aren't sure of the love that He has toward *you?* I promise, it is easier to love others when you know how much you are loved.

God's love is what makes Christianity different from

every other religion. No one else's god loves them as our God loves mankind.

Once I heard a Christian minister tell a story about being in a foreign country and having a debate with the leader of another religion. Both the Christian and the other leader pulled out their books and argued with each other about which religion was correct.

In the midst of the argument the Spirit of God spoke to the heart of the Christian minister and said, "Ask him if his god loves him." The question stopped the other leader cold. The argument was over, because he couldn't answer yes. Everything about God is about His love for you!

It was His love that caused Him to plan our redemption from the moment Adam and Eve ate the forbidden fruit in the Garden of Eden. It was because of love that Jesus came to the earth to die a horrible death and pay the price for our sin.

Everything about God is
about His love for you!

The Bible doesn't say God sent Jesus because He was angry with mankind. It says, "For God *so loved* the world that He gave His only begotten Son, that whoever believes in Him should not perish but have everlasting life" (John 3:16, emphasis added).

God Is Love

This love is the very essence of God. His love is what motivates Him in every interaction with you. First John 4:8 says that God *is* love. He doesn't *have* love as you and I do. He *is* love. His very being is love. His response to everything is motivated by love, even when He is correcting you. This love is always looking out for what is best for you.

The Bible says that He put that love in your heart when you were saved and His Spirit came to reside in you (Rom. 5:5). There was a time when I thought love was one of God's topics. I thought it was on the list of topics alongside salvation, healing, provision, and protection. But the longer I've known Him, the more I've come to realize that all these blessings come to us *because* of His love. It is not one of His topics—it is Him! Every one of His blessings and provisions comes because of His love.

In other words, He saved you because He loves you. He heals you because He loves you! He provides for and protects you because He loves you.

God's love changes everything. It changes the way you pray. When you realize how much He loves you, you don't have to approach Him with a begging attitude. You don't need to say, "O God, please heal me! Please meet my needs! Please protect me!" When you really know that His only motivation toward you is love, you can say, "Father, of course You'll heal me—You love me! Of course You'll protect me—You love me!" This is a supernatural, unconditional, agape love that changes your life.

But you must believe it. Galatians 5:6 says that faith works by love. I like to say it this way: faith works by *knowing how much you're loved.* If you don't know, you might still be approaching God and begging. When you know how much He loves you, you can approach Him with faith, knowing you have your answer from a loving heavenly Father because He has promised it.

You Can Be Sure

Too many Christians aren't sure about God. They aren't sure if they can count on Him, nor do they know what He will do in a given situation. They're not sure of His love for them. They know *about* Him, but they don't *know* Him.

Here is an example. Let's say you need five hundred dollars, so I hand you a piece of paper with a telephone number on it and tell you, "Call my dad. He'll give you the money." You might be desperate enough to make the call and say, "Well, Karen told me to call you and ask." But you still wouldn't *know for sure* what my dad would say. Why? Because you don't know him.

> This is a supernatural, unconditional,
> agape love that changes your life.

But if *I*—his only daughter, the apple of his eye—were to call and ask him for five hundred dollars, I know what he would say. Why? Because I know him. I've known him all my life. I know he loves me and would do anything to help me. I have daughter status with him.

Many people approach God the way they might approach my father—with caution. They pray, but they're just not sure about the reception they'll get. They don't *know* for sure that He loves them and would do anything for them.

If that's you, I pray you can increase your capacity to be loved by God. I pray that you can get to a place of *knowing*. First John 4:16 says, "And we have *known and believed* the love that God has for us. God is love, and he who abides in love abides in God, and God in him" (emphasis added).

This is the key, knowing and believing the love. How do you get to a place of knowing and believing? You get there by meditating on God's truths until they seem more real than your feelings, experience, or circumstances. Many people believe that God has the power and ability to help them; they're just not sure if He will. They question His love.

There is a story in the Bible about someone who wasn't sure about Jesus. Mark 1:40 says, "Now a leper came to Him, imploring Him, kneeling down to Him and saying to Him, 'If You are willing, You can make me clean.'"

This leper had heard about Jesus. He knew that Jesus could heal, which is why he came to Him. But it is obvious that he just wasn't quite sure if Jesus would heal him.

Thankfully, out of His great mercy, Jesus did heal him. The next verse says, "Then Jesus, moved with compassion, stretched out His hand and touched him, and said to him, 'I am willing; be cleansed'" (Mark 1:41).

Many people feel the way that leper did. They approach God because they've heard that He can do miracles, but they don't know for sure that He'll do one for them. They come with a big *if* in their minds, just as the leper did. I heard one minister say, "*If* is the badge of doubt." And the Bible tells us we can't receive anything from God if we doubt (James 1:6).

It doesn't matter how much power and ability someone possesses—if you're not convinced he will use the power for you, you can't have faith to receive it. What good does all the power in the world do you if you're not sure it will work for you? That was the problem with the leper. He questioned God's love for him.

Don't let that be the problem in your life. Don't let there be any question in your mind about your Father's amazing, unconditional love for you. Make a new resolve to understand His love toward you in a greater way, and let Him love you.

What Is Your Response?

The good news of the gospel is not that Christians are to be committed to God; rather it is that He is committed to us. It is not about what you are supposed to do for Him, but about what He has done for you through Jesus.

> Many people believe that God has the power and ability to help them; they're just not sure if He will.

Yes, we believe in being committed to God, being dedicated to Him, and serving Him. After all, the Bible says you are not your own, but you were bought with a price (1 Cor. 6:19–20). But doing good and living a life that pleases the Lord is meant to be your response to the gospel.

We're often told to love God, serve God, and be committed to God without really understanding who it is that we're serving and what He's done for us. When you see what God has done for you and just how dedicated and committed His love is toward you, it causes you to reciprocate. The way to love God fully is to understand *how much He loves you.*

Don't get me wrong, His love isn't a license to go around sinning or doing whatever your flesh wants to do. Romans 6:1–2 says, "What shall we say then? Shall we continue in sin that grace may abound? Certainly not! How shall we who died to sin live any longer in it?"

Your response to God's great love shouldn't be, "God loves me no matter what, so I can do whatever I want," or, "How much can I get away with and still go to heaven?" His Word has much to say about living right and becoming a mature Christian after you're saved. Rather His love allows your response to be, "Father, You love me so much and You've given Your all for me that I love You too and want to please You."

I want God to be pleased with me. Don't you? He has blessed me so much, I want to order my life according to His way. When I obey Him and follow His instructions, life goes better. Have you ever noticed that? When you obey Him, you can expect peace.

On the other hand, if you disobey God, you can expect trouble. He will still love you, but disobedience has a cost. When a child disobeys or acts badly, he is still a son; he is still in relationship with his parents, with all the rights and privileges of sonship in that family. But disobedience can jeopardize his fellowship with his parents and can also cause tension and consequences. He'll have to be corrected. Through all that, however, his parents still love him and still count him as their son. It is the same with God and His children. You have to get it out of your head that God loves you based on what you do (or don't do).

You don't do good to be good. Mankind tried that approach under the old covenant, and it became quite obvious that it doesn't work. You're good only because of the price that was paid for you. It was Jesus's blood, not your perfect behavior, that cleansed you of your sin. (See Hebrews 9:26.) Now you're the righteousness of God *in Him* (2 Cor. 5:21), not because of what you've done, but because of what Jesus has done.

You couldn't earn or deserve salvation—you simply received it by faith, believing what Jesus did for you. Ephesians 2:8 says, "For by grace you have been saved through faith, and that not of yourselves; it is the gift of God."

<hr>

> You have to get it out of your
> head that God loves you based
> on what you do (or don't do).

<hr>

When you received Jesus as Lord of your life, you received the forgiveness of sin and moved into right standing before God (Col. 1:14; Rom. 3:21–24). Now you are to walk a holy, disciplined life worthy of the calling you have been given (Eph. 4:1). However, if you slip along the way, God never stops loving you. He loves you *unconditionally*.

Natural human love always has conditions attached

to it. It says: "I love you if you love me." "I love you if you treat me right." "I love you if you make me happy." But once someone stops making you happy, you might stop loving him. That's *not* the same as agape love, the God kind of love. His love is not based on what you do. God loves you because *He is love.*

There Is Proof of God's Love in His Word

You can't come into a deeper revelation of God's love without His Word. Here are seven proofs from the Bible that He loves you. Meditate on these until they become real to you.

Proof #1: *Before He lived in you, He longed to be closer to you.*

Under the old covenant the presence of God on earth was in a box called the ark of the covenant (Exod. 25:10–22; Lev. 16:2). This ark was located in the tabernacle, behind the veil in what was called the holy of holies. No man could approach it, except the high priest who could go in once a year, on a special day called the Day of Atonement (Lev. 23:27). The idea was that a sinful man could not approach a holy God.

The tabernacle was in the center of the Israelites' camp or city because God wanted to be in the center of their lives. The word *tabernacle* means "a dwelling place."[1] God didn't want to be far away from His people. He wanted to dwell right with them.

But when God was planning His new covenant with mankind, He must have decided: "I don't want to just be in the center of their camp, I want to be even closer—I want to be in them, in the center of their being. I want to be in their hearts, as they are in Mine."

God spoke through Jeremiah saying, "Then I will give them a heart to know Me, that I am the LORD; and they shall be My people, and I will be their God, for they shall return to Me with their whole heart....I will put My law in their minds, and write it on their hearts; and I will be their God, and they shall be My people" (Jer. 24:7; 31:33).

Now, Jeremiah was talking to a rebellious people whose disobedience was about to cause them to be defeated by their enemies and taken away to foreign lands as prisoners, exiled from the Promised Land of Canaan. It wasn't a happy time in Israel's history.

But despite their rebellion, you can hear the heart of a loving Father, crying out, telling His people that there would come a time when they would be reunited in heart and mind. God says, "Yes, I have loved you with an everlasting love; therefore with lovingkindness I have drawn you" (Jer. 31:3). And when God says "everlasting," He really means it.

God loves you because *He is love.*

If God declared His never-failing, unconditional love for a rebellious and disobedient people, how does He feel about *you*, His child bought by the blood of Jesus? Before the new covenant was ever in place, He wanted to be even closer to you than He had been to the Israelites. So He was making plans to write His laws on your heart by putting His Spirit right inside you. He loves you!

Proof #2: *God knew you would never deserve forgiveness, so He made a way for you.*

The Bible says that God showed how much He loves you by sending Jesus to save you when you couldn't save yourself: "God demonstrates His own love toward us, in that while we were still sinners, Christ died for us" (Rom. 5:8).

God knew that you would never be good enough on your own and that you could never earn your way back into fellowship with Him. You could never do enough to attain admittance to heaven. Therefore, out of His great love, He sent His Son to make a way for us. He loved you first—before you were ever made righteous!

God didn't require that you prove yourself worthy; He just grabbed you into His arms despite your lost and dying condition and saved you. He proved His love to you before you ever had an opportunity to do anything for Him: "In this is love, not that we loved God, but that He loved us and sent His Son to be the propitiation for our sins" (1 John 4:10).

God's Word makes it clear:

> But God, who is rich in mercy, because of His great love with which He loved us, even when we were dead in trespasses, made us alive together with Christ (by grace you have been saved), and raised us up together, and made us sit together in the heavenly places in Christ Jesus, that in the ages to come He might show the exceeding riches of His grace in His kindness toward us in Christ Jesus.
>
> —Ephesians 2:4–7

God wants to show off in you, not because of anything you've done (or haven't done), but because of His great mercy and His great love for you.

Proof #3: *He gave to you.*

God didn't just shout down from heaven, "I love you!" No, instead He sent His Son. He committed Himself to you, in the flesh. John 3:16 says, "God so loved the world that He gave His only begotten Son." First John 4:9 says, "This is how God showed his love for us: God sent his only Son into the world so we might live through him" (THE MESSAGE).

Sometimes people feel as if God is holding back from them, thinking that He could do more. By sending Jesus, God gave His best for you. He didn't hold anything back!

Romans 8:32 says, "He who did not spare His own Son, but delivered Him up for us all, how shall He not with Him also freely give us all things?"

He loved you first—before you
were ever made righteous!

Read that again. If God was going to hold anything back from you, it would have been His precious Son. I have sons. I've tried on this idea in my head: Could I give my son for you (or for anyone)? That would be a sacrifice! In giving Jesus, God has proven beyond any doubt that He will freely give you anything. He loves you. Don't doubt it or question it.

Proof #4: *God thinks you're the most valuable thing around.*

The Bible says, "You were not redeemed with corruptible things, like silver or gold…but with the precious blood of Christ, as of a lamb without blemish and without spot" (1 Pet. 1:18–19).

Notice that God calls silver and gold "corruptible," meaning something that could disintegrate or become tainted. That is *not* what I think of when I think of silver or gold. Do you?

If I were come to your house with two suitcases, one full of silver and the other full of gold, and open them in your living room, you probably wouldn't look in and say, "Ah, corruptible." No, you'd probably say, "May I have some?" Because you would look at the silver and gold and think, "*Valuable!*"

By contrast God said He needed something *more* precious (valuable) than gold or silver to buy you. He needed something that would never change, disintegrate, or decrease in value. And there was only one thing that met those requirements: the blood of His only Son.

It is said that the value of something is determined by the price that was paid for it. Think of an auction. If a ring sells for one thousand dollars in one round, but a necklace goes for ten thousand dollars in the next round, we would say that the necklace is *more valuable* because the higher price was paid for it.

Following this logic, you can conclude that *humans* must be the most valuable things on the planet, because the highest price was paid for them.

Don't believe the lies of the devil when he says you're not worth much. The highest price was paid for you.

Proof #5: *God is paying attention.*

Matthew 10:29–30 says, "Are not two sparrows sold for a copper coin? And not one of them falls to the ground apart from your Father's will. But the very hairs of your head are all numbered."

Take a minute to think about this passage. God knows how many hairs are on your head. In fact, He knows how many hairs are on my head and on every other head on the planet! According to the last count of the world census at the time of my writing this book, there are roughly seven billion heads in the world.

And here is another thought: This morning, when you were getting dressed and fixing your hair for the day, did a few hairs fall out? That happened to me. And that must mean that God keeps a running count of the hairs on my head and on all seven billion other heads! Just when I think I have God all figured out or that He's only into the big stuff, here's proof that He's paying attention to the smallest details in our lives.

> By sending Jesus, God gave
> His best for you. He didn't
> hold anything back!

I mean, if you were in a relationship with someone who was counting the hairs on your head, I would tell you to run for your life, because that is obsession! But your Father is obsessed with you, and only in a good way. For all the questions you've had and all the times you might have felt like He wasn't paying attention, I'm here to tell you that He *is* paying attention. He loves you. He is paying such close attention to you, He not only is

counting the hairs on your head but *He also hears you.*
When you talk, He is listening.

Psalm 40:1 says, "I waited patiently for the LORD; and
He inclined to me, and heard my cry." When I read the
word "inclined," I picture God leaning over from His
throne to listen. He hears me! And He hears you too.
Psalm 34:4 says, "I sought the LORD, and He heard me,
and delivered me from all my fears."

Does it matter that God hears you? I think it makes
all the difference. If He didn't hear you when you called
out to Him, how could He deliver you from all of your
fears? It would be like calling a company's customer service number and getting transferred from recording to
recording until you hang up in frustration, knowing that
no one at the company heard you. That is *not* a satisfac-
tory phone call.

There are people who feel as if God is like that customer service call, that He doesn't hear them when they
pray. What a hopeless feeling that must be. But that is
not what the Bible says about prayer or God; rather, it
says He hears you! And that makes all the difference.
First John 5:14 says, "Now this is the confidence that
we have in Him, that if we ask anything according to
His will, He hears us. And if we know that He hears us,
whatever we ask, we know that we have the petitions
that we have asked of Him."

Knowing that God hears you gives you confidence
that your prayer is being answered. If you thought He
wasn't listening, you would never be able to believe. In
fact, you would conclude that it is fruitless to talk with
Him. That would be true hopelessness. But fear not;

God repeatedly promises in His Word that He is listening to you!

Proof #6: *God calls you His own son or daughter.*

First John 3:1 says, "See how very much our Father loves us, for he calls us his children, and that is what we are!" (NLT). Think about it: children have different privileges at home than guests do. Guests have to ring the doorbell; sons and daughters just walk right into the house without knocking. Guests have to wait to be served food; children just go to the refrigerator or cupboards and help themselves.

You are God's son or daughter. You're His kid! He calls you son or daughter (2 Cor. 6:18). He doesn't call you servant, slave, acquaintance, associate, or neighbor. He calls you son or daughter, and as such you're accepted in a way that others are not, with rights and privileges only a child of His household can lay claim to.

> Humans must be the most valuable
> things on the planet, because the
> highest price was paid for them.

When it comes to solving your problems, God doesn't look at you as just another item on His to-do list. In reality He gives you personal attention, because you're a member of His family. A father is responsible for members of his family in a way that he's not responsible for his associates or neighbors.

I like how the J. B. Phillips version translates 1 Peter 5:7: "You can throw the whole weight of your anxieties upon him, for you are his personal concern." You are God's personal concern. He loves you.

Proof #7: *God has given you access.*

Hebrews 4:16 says, "Let us therefore come boldly to the throne of grace, that we may obtain mercy and find grace to help in time of need." You don't have to crawl on your belly into the presence of God; rather, He tells you to come *boldly* because you have access right into His throne room.

Under the old covenant, no one could go into the presence of God except the high priest, and even he could go in only once a year (Exod. 30:10; Heb. 9:7). Sin separated humans from God. But now that the blood of Jesus has been accepted as a sacrifice for sin, and He has torn the veil that separated man from God (Mark 15:38), you have complete access to the throne. You can approach Him boldly as His child. You'll never be shut out or turned away.

You are completely accepted in the Beloved (Eph. 1:6). The access you now have to God reminds me of a scene in the movie *Anna and the King*. This film tells the story of a widowed British woman, Anna, who taught school many years ago in Siam (now Thailand) to the king's children. One day during class a fight broke out between her son and the king's oldest son, the heir to the throne. The king's youngest and favorite child, a little girl about five years old, ran from the classroom to tell her father about the fight.

The king was in his throne room, with hundreds of people waiting for an audience with him, and only one at a time was allowed to approach him with their request.

The rest of the people were lined up in rows, bowing down to the king, their faces to the floor. Royal protocol called for their heads to be lower than the king's, and none of them would dare approach the throne without being asked, on penalty of death.

But when the little princess entered the huge room, she completely ignored all the people who had been bowing down for hours. Instead she just scampered down the aisle right past them. She ran right up to her daddy on the throne and began to whisper in his ear!

Did the king call for his guards to haul her away or behead her? Of course not. He leaned down and listened patiently to her breathless story about the fight, then picked her up and carried her back down the aisle toward the classroom, leaving all his subjects still bowing with their faces to the floor.

That little princess came boldly to the throne because she knew she had access. She was her father's favorite and had no fear of approaching him when she needed him.

> You're accepted in a way that others are not, with rights and privileges only a child of his household can lay claim to.

This scene paints a perfect picture of you and your heavenly Father. You are completely accepted and loved by Him. You can approach the throne and whisper in His ear anytime you want! You have access, and He loves you.

The Bible has even more proofs of your Father's perfect

love for you. I have included these seven to help get you started and to give you a *knowing* that you are loved. I encourage you to bathe your spirit in these truths and keep them cooking on a front burner. That is the way to *know and believe* the love that God has for you.

Now Engage

You are deeply loved by God. Meditate on and declare these truths from God's Word to build your confidence in His great love for you.

Front-Burner Truth: "I know I am unconditionally loved by my Father God."

> For I am persuaded that neither death nor life, nor angels nor principalities nor powers, nor things present nor things to come, nor height nor depth, nor any other created thing, shall be able to separate us from the love of God which is in Christ Jesus our Lord.
> —ROMANS 8:38–39

My heavenly Father loves me! I've never been loved like this before. His love for me never stops or fades out because of something I did (or didn't do). It doesn't stop because of something that happened (or hasn't happened). This love comes from the heart of God. It's not based on my goodness; it's based on *His* goodness. I cannot be separated from His love.

> I will put My law in their minds, and write it on their hearts; and I will be their God, and they shall be My people.
> —JEREMIAH 31:33

I am the recipient of God's redemption plan. He loved me so much He gave me a better covenant in Christ, based on better promises, and put His Spirit right inside me—in my mind and in my heart! He is my God and I am His beloved. He loves me with a never-failing, unconditional love.

> God demonstrates His own love toward us, in that while we were still sinners, Christ died for us.
> —ROMANS 5:8

God knew that I'd never be good enough on my own— that I could never earn my way back into fellowship with Him or do right enough to attain heaven. So out of His great love He sent His Son to do right for me. Before I was ever made righteous, He loved me first. He grabbed me up in my lost and dying condition and saved me.

> He who did not spare His own Son, but delivered Him up for us all, how shall He not with Him also freely give us all things?
> —ROMANS 8:32

You can approach Him boldly
as His child. You'll never be
shut out or turned away.

God is not holding anything back from me. If He was going to hold anything back, it would have been His only Son. But He gave His best for me. He didn't just shout down from heaven, "I love you!" No, He sent Jesus. He committed Himself to me, in the flesh. He's proven beyond a shadow of a doubt that He'll freely give me anything.

> You were not redeemed with corruptible things, like silver or gold...but with the precious blood of Christ, as of a lamb without blemish and without spot.
> —1 PETER 1:18–19

God thought that silver and gold wasn't enough to buy me. He used something *more* precious (valuable) than silver or gold—something that would never change, disintegrate, or decrease in value: the blood of His only Son. I will never again believe the lies of the devil when he says I'm not worth much, because God paid the highest price for me.

> Now this is the confidence that we have in Him, that if we ask anything according to His will, He hears us. And if we know that He hears us, whatever we ask, we know that we have the petitions that we have asked of Him.
> —1 JOHN 5:14–15

God is paying attention to me. Every time I call out to Him, He listens and hears me. He even has the hairs on my head numbered! I have His undivided attention whenever I want it.

> See how very much our Father loves us, for he calls us his children, and that is what we are!
> —1 JOHN 3:1, NLT

As God's own child I lay claim to all the rights and privileges that children have. I am not a guest or a servant or a neighbor. I'm His child, accepted in His household in ways that others aren't. When it comes to solving my problems, I'm not just another number on God's list of things to do. He gives me His personal attention, because I'm a member of His family.

> Let us therefore come boldly to the throne of grace, that we may obtain mercy and find grace to help in time of need.
> —HEBREWS 4:16

God loves me so much He has given me direct access to Him at all times. I don't have to crawl on my belly into His presence; I approach Him boldly, as His child. I'll never be shut out or turned away. I am completely accepted in the Beloved (Eph. 1:6). I can run and whisper in His ear anytime I want to! I am confident in His love for me.

Chapter Ten

GOD STILL THINKS YOU'RE COMING OUT ON TOP

ERE IS ANOTHER front-burner truth: God still thinks you're coming out on top. He believes the best of you. He always causes you to triumph (2 Cor. 2:14). My sons and I have lived out this truth. We have a saying in our family when trouble comes: "If anyone's going to come out on top in this situation, it's going to be us!" We are all serving God in the full-time ministry today, strengthened by His goodness and His mercy toward us. God knows how to take horrible things that have happened to you and make them turn out good.

Romans 8:28 is one of the theme verses of my life: "And we know that all things work together for good to those who love God, to those who are the called according to His purpose." Yes, all things. Notice it doesn't say all things *are* good. It says that God knows how to take even the horrible things and work them out for good. If it is not good yet, then the story just isn't over!

The key lies in the first three words of the verse, "And we *know*." You have to know (believe) that God will bring you out of your troubles and you will come out on top. You get that *knowing* from His Word. So let's look at some Bible passages.

Joseph Had Trouble From the Start

The story of Joseph is one that shows how someone can go through trouble—one really horrible situation after another—and come out on top. It is one of my favorite stories.

God knows how to take horrible
things that have happened to you
and make them turn out good.

Joseph's father was a man named Israel (aka Jacob), who was a descendant of Abraham and therefore an heir of God's covenant. Israel had twelve sons, and they became the twelve tribes of Israel. Joseph was the second youngest.

In this story there was trouble from the beginning. The Bible says, "Now Israel loved Joseph more than all his children, because he was the son of his old age. Also he made him a tunic [coat] of many colors" (Gen. 37:3).

It is a bad idea to love one of your children more than the others. Favoritism causes all kinds of trouble. For starters we get a picture of Joseph strutting around in his coat of many colors, daily flaunting in his brothers' faces that he was their dad's favorite.

You can imagine what his ten older brothers thought of that. Genesis 37:4 says, "When his brothers saw that their father loved him more than all his brothers, they hated him and could not speak peaceably to him." There was some major sibling rivalry going on in this household.

One day young Joseph had a dream from God, and he told it to his brothers. He dreamed that he and his brothers were all sheaves (stalks of wheat bound up into bundles) in a field. Except that the sheaf representing Joseph himself stood upright, and all the other sheaves (his brothers) bowed down to him! (See Genesis 37:5–7.)

Can you imagine how well that went over? Joseph's brothers said to him, "'Shall you indeed reign over us? Or shall you indeed have dominion over us?' So they hated him even more for his dreams and for his words" (Gen. 37:8).

If that wasn't enough, Joseph had *another* dream, and this time the sun, the moon, and eleven stars all bowed down to him. Even his father disliked that dream and rebuked him for it. The brothers, of course, were livid. So one day when Israel sent Joseph to check on his older brothers in the field, the brothers hatched a plan. They stripped off Joseph's coat, threw him in a pit, and sold him to some traders from a neighboring country who happened to be traveling by. The brothers then sloshed some goat's blood on the beautiful coat, took it home to their father, and let him think that Joseph had been killed by a wild beast. Joseph, meanwhile, was taken to Egypt and resold into slavery.

Think about what happened in this story. It is easy to see why Joseph's brothers didn't like him, but usually, when push comes to shove, even if your brothers don't like you, you expect them to watch your back. Instead, these brothers sold Joseph into slavery. And he was just seventeen years old. I can't imagine what Joseph must have been feeling. He was betrayed by his brothers in the most devastating and humiliating way possible, bound hand and foot, and then taken to a country far from his home. It is likely that he was not treated kindly at all before being resold as a slave in a country where he probably didn't speak the language, at least at first.

Since Joseph had been his father's favorite back home, he may have never made a bed or swept a floor in his life, but suddenly he was a slave! He had no rights, no privileges, no one to stand up for him or even care about him. And there was no chance of ever going free. He must have been terrified. Joseph was in trouble.

Watch Your Attitude

If I found myself in the same predicament as Joseph, I might have felt sorry for myself. I might have cried for the first month or two. But apparently that is not what Joseph did. The first thing we read about his experience as a slave comes in Genesis 39:2: "The LORD was with Joseph, and he was a successful man; and he was in the house of his master the Egyptian." Now I don't know about you, but when I think "slave," I *don't* think "successful man."

But that is what the Bible says. And look at that. It says "the LORD was with Joseph." In my mind it seems that if the Lord is with you, then you *won't* be betrayed by your brothers and get sold into slavery! Obviously there was something supernatural going on. Joseph was in the worst trouble of his life, but he was successful and God was with him! Maybe you're in the worst trouble of your life right now. I'm telling you, God still thinks you're coming out on top! There is more to the story.

We don't see many details of Joseph's daily life as a slave, but consider what he must have been doing in order to be successful. Do you think he stayed in bed long hours every morning, feeling sorry for himself? Did he cry and wring his hands all day long, mourning over all he had lost, wishing he was home and planning revenge on his brothers? Did he have a bad attitude and snap at everyone around him in his captivity?

I am guessing that he didn't do any of these things. The Bible says, "And his master saw that the LORD was with him.... Then he made him overseer of his house, and all that he had he put under his [Joseph's] authority" (Gen. 39:3–4). Someone as smart as Potiphar, captain of Pharaoh's guard, wouldn't just put a teenage kid in charge of his whole household unless that kid had some good skills.

My guess is that Joseph was up early every day, working hard, using his God-given organizational skills in ways that benefited the household—yes, the household of his *captor*. He probably had a good attitude about it, because he ran this house smoothly and he was the boss of the other slaves. It's likely that most of the people under his leadership were older than he was, yet they listened to him. The supernatural was working for Joseph, but he had to do his part in the natural too.

Every time I read this story of Joseph, I have to check up on myself. In the face of being betrayed by loved ones, being exiled from my home, and being sold into slavery with no hope of freedom ever again, would I rise up the way Joseph did? Would I remember the dream in my heart (that everyone would eventually bow down) and not only keep going but also excel in the midst of trouble? Would I have a good attitude?

Because Joseph was living under the old covenant, he didn't even have the Holy Spirit of God *living inside him* as you do. With your "better covenant, which was established on better promises" (Heb. 8:6), how much more can you excel in the midst of trouble?

Be Alert in Times of Trouble

Do you ever feel as if lots of troubles are stacking up against you? Do you ever grow anxious because you have more headaches and heartaches than you can handle? If so, then you will be able to relate to what happened next in Joseph's story. Even though things were going pretty well for him in Potiphar's house, his troubles were far from over.

Our young friend was a handsome fellow. Genesis 39:7 says, "His master's wife cast longing eyes on Joseph, and she said, 'Lie with me.'" Joseph did what was right; day after day he fended off the advances of his master's wife. Of course, this made her mad. So she lied about him, saying he attacked her, and just that quickly Joseph found himself thrown into prison (vv. 8–20).

> Do you ever feel as if lots of troubles
> are stacking up against you?

Joseph did the right and honorable thing, but he wound up in prison! In those days when a slave was incarcerated, there was no phone call to a lawyer. There was no trial. There were no character witnesses or an opportunity to present a defense. Joseph was in prison for life.

I can't even imagine how he must have felt. Talk about a hopeless situation! Again, Joseph could have easily melted into a heap and felt sorry for himself. He could have gotten bitter. Or given up.

Maybe you've been in a similar situation, a place where you were doing the right thing, obeying God, making the best of bad circumstances, and still you were blindsided. When that happens, it is easy to get bitter or give up.

But look at how Joseph responded: "But the LORD was with Joseph and showed him mercy, and He gave him favor in the sight of the keeper of the prison. And the keeper of the prison committed to Joseph's hand all the prisoners who were in the prison; whatever they did there, it was his doing" (Gen 39:21–22).

Joseph came out on top again. Despite a horrible situation, he rose up, used his gifts, and was promoted. He kept the dreams God had given him alive in his heart. If he could do that then, we can also do it now!

There Is a Way Out

Joseph was going about the everyday business of running the prison when the butler and the baker from the palace both were thrown into his cellblock. They had offended Pharaoh. Soon after they arrived, both men had dreams, and no one except Joseph could interpret the meaning. (See Genesis 40.)

Joseph told the butler that his dream meant he would be restored to service, but the baker's dream meant that he would have his head chopped off. Joseph was correct. It happened just that way. Just before the butler headed back to Pharaoh's chambers, happy and free, Joseph asked him, "'Remember me when it is well with you, and please show kindness to me; make mention of me to Pharaoh, and get me out of this house [prison]. For indeed I was stolen away from the land of the Hebrews; and also I have done nothing here that they should put me into the dungeon'" (Gen. 40:14–15).

> He kept the dream alive in his heart. If he could do that then, we can also do it now!

Here was a chance for Joseph to get rescued, a miraculous way out. I can imagine that he had great hope that now someone on the outside would speak for him, and he might be released. The first few days after the butler's departure were probably filled with hope, as Joseph imagined all the things he would do when he got out of prison.

But no word came. I can only imagine how Joseph's hope must have waned as day after day, then week after week went by. For most people, after so many months of waiting, all hope would be gone, and despair would have set in. The Bible said the butler forgot about Joseph, and *two full years* went by (Gen. 40:23; 41:1). Here was another chance for Joseph to become discouraged beyond belief. Yet the dream God had given him hadn't changed, and he kept it alive in his heart.

Victory Does Come

One day something wonderful finally happened. Pharaoh himself had two dreams, and no one could interpret them. At that moment the butler remembered Joseph. He told Pharaoh there was a man in prison who could interpret dreams.

Joseph was summoned to the palace, and he interpreted the dreams, revealing that there would be seven years of plenty in the land of Egypt, followed by seven years of famine. Joseph went on to deliver the word of the Lord to Pharaoh concerning the dreams: "'Now therefore, let Pharaoh select a discerning and wise man, and set him over the land of Egypt'" (Gen. 41:33).

Guess who Pharaoh chose as administrator over the land of Egypt? That is right; he chose Joseph! The Bible says, "Then Pharaoh took his signet ring off his hand and put it on Joseph's hand; and he clothed him in garments of fine linen and put a gold chain around his neck. And he had him ride in the second chariot which he had; and they cried out before him, 'Bow the knee!' So he set him over all the land of Egypt" (Gen. 41:42–43).

After years of suffering through betrayal, loneliness, hard work, and imprisonment, in one day Joseph moved from the prison to the palace and became the second in command over all of Egypt!

Through diligence, persistence, and faith Joseph came out on top. And that is not the end of the story either. Joseph's initial dreams didn't come true until several years later when his brothers traveled from Israel during the famine. They asked him for food, and they bowed down to him many times (Gen. 42:6).

Was Joseph angry with his brothers? No. He forgave them for betraying him, declaring, "'You meant evil against me; but God meant it for good, in order to bring it about as it is this day, to save many people alive'" (Gen. 50:20). Joseph's obedience and perseverance ended up saving his family and most of the known world during the famine.

In one day Joseph moved
from the prison to the palace
and became second in
command over all of Egypt!

God knows exactly how to take evil and work it for good. Joseph's dreams obviously helped him keep a heavenly perspective of his circumstances. He was a poster child for the saying, "You can't keep a good man down." He never gave up, never got mad at God. He continued to rise up, use his gifts, and make the best of every situation. Joseph came out on top, and he brought many people with him. If he could do it, you can too!

Rejoice!

As I have noted, when my husband died, I had to take over as pastor of our church. I had a wonderful staff to help me, but at first, the responsibility weighed me down, and I didn't have a clear vision of coming out on top. I identified with Paul when he talked about the daily pressures and anxieties of taking care of churches (2 Cor. 11:28).

Reading about Paul always helped. When you think your life might be hard, you need to read about Paul too.

> I've worked much harder, been jailed more often, beaten up more times than I can count, and at death's door time after time. I've been flogged five times with the Jews' thirty-nine lashes, beaten by Roman rods three times, pummeled with rocks once. I've been shipwrecked three times, and immersed in the open sea for a night and a day. In hard traveling year in and year out, I've had to ford rivers, fend off robbers, struggle with friends, struggle with foes. I've been at risk in the city, at risk in the country, endangered by desert sun and sea storm, and betrayed by those I thought were my brothers. I've known drudgery and hard labor, many a long and lonely night without sleep, many a missed meal, blasted by the cold, naked to the weather. And that's not the half of it, when you throw in the daily pressures and anxieties of all the churches. When someone gets to the end of his rope, I feel the desperation in my bones. When someone is duped into sin, an angry fire burns in my gut.
> —2 CORINTHIANS 11:23–29,
> THE MESSAGE

I have been through a lot, but I have never been through anything similar to what Paul went through. Have you? Yet despite the hardships, setbacks, and persecution he faced, this is the same man who said, "Rejoice in the Lord always. Again I will say, rejoice!" (Phil. 4:4). Do you know where Paul *was* when he wrote that verse? In prison!

If anyone mastered the skill of coming out on top

in the midst of adverse circumstances, it was Paul. All those horrible ordeals listed in 1 Corinthians 11, and then he rejoices.

> When you think your life might be
> hard, you need to read about Paul.

He responded like that more than once. Acts 16:24–26 recounts the time when he and Silas were beaten, imprisoned, and bound in stocks for preaching the gospel. At midnight (the darkest hour), when they were praising God and all the prisoners were listening, a great earthquake shook the prison and everyone's chains were loosed.

Paul knew that releasing God's power through praise would enable him to come out on top. Apparently praising God in times of trouble can help everyone *around* you get free too! I think the more we read about Paul, the more we can react as he did in horrible situations. I encourage you to dig into the Word and study Paul's life. Learn all you can from his admonition to *rejoice*, and then try it in your own life. I am confident that you'll see some amazing results. I have.

Come Through the Fire

The Bible is packed with great stories about going through trying circumstances and coming out on top. Remember our friends Shadrach, Meshach, and Abednego who wouldn't eat the king's food? They lived adventurous lives. Not only did they get the victory over that situation, but they also got into big trouble later when they refused to bow down to a statue of King Nebuchadnezzar. (See Daniel 1–3.)

At that time, by national decree, everyone in the kingdom of Babylon was required to bow down to the king's statue: "'Whoever does not fall down and worship shall be cast immediately into the midst of a burning fiery furnace'" (Dan. 3:6).

When it was reported to Nebuchadnezzar that these three Hebrew boys wouldn't comply, he was furious and commanded that they be thrown into a furnace, heated *seven times hotter* than normal (v. 19). Now I think that is funny. Wasn't the regular temperature of the furnace hot enough to burn up human bodies? The devil loves to make situations appear to be more dire than they really are—he loves to turn up the heat! What a liar.

It was so hot that when the furnace door was opened, the heat coming from inside killed the strong soldiers who had bound the three friends and cast them into the flames (v. 22). That's really hot!

Have you ever had the heat turned up? Have you ever faced a setback that looked as if you would lose everything? The pressure can be intense. Yet when faced with a life-threatening situation, these young boys had faith in their God. They refused to worship anyone but Him and had even told Nebuchadnezzar, "Our God whom we serve is able to deliver us from the burning fiery furnace, and He will deliver us from your hand, O king" (v. 17).

A little while after ordering that the three be thrown in the furnace, Nebuchadnezzar went to check on the progress. He looked into the furnace, and said, "I see four men loose, walking in the midst of the fire; and they are not hurt, and the form of the fourth is like the Son of God" (v. 25).

Now that is coming out on top even though the situation looked hopeless. Those young men weren't even hurt! When they came out of the furnace the hairs on their head were not singed, their clothes weren't burned, and they didn't even smell like smoke (v. 27)! Nothing from that experience stuck to them.

> The devil loves to make situations
> appear to be more dire than
> they really are—he loves to
> turn up the heat! What a liar.

What a testimony! We're still talking about Shadrach, Meshach, and Abednego today. God knew how to bring those young men out on top, and He knows how to bring *you* out on top, no matter how the devil has tried to turn up the heat on you.

When you obey God, listen to His voice, and follow His lead, you too can walk away not even smelling like smoke. And those who stood by watching will be telling your testimony for a *long* time. To God be the glory!

You Don't Need to Worry

Neither Joseph nor the three Hebrew boys wasted any time *worrying.* In order for you to keep believing that God is going to bring you out on top, you're going to have to stop worrying. I know, this sounds easier said than done. But it is vital. God doesn't want you to worry.

Besides, worrying is fruitless. It doesn't solve one problem or help anyone. Chances are good that you can't even remember everything you were worrying about one year ago. Leo F. Buscaglia once said, "Worry never robs tomorrow of its sorrow, it only saps today of its joy."[1] Corrie ten Boom put it this way: "Worrying is carrying tomorrow's load with today's strength, carrying two days at once. It is moving into tomorrow ahead of time. Worrying doesn't empty tomorrow of its sorrow, it empties today of its strength."[2] And I heard someone else say, "A truckload of worry will not pay an ounce of debt." Isn't that the truth!

You can't worry and be walking in faith at the same time. It is impossible. What are you worried about right now? Set your questions and concerns on a back burner. Now look at what God's Word says about worry:

> Therefore I tell you, stop being perpetually uneasy (anxious and worried) about your life, what you shall eat or what you shall drink; or about your body, what you shall put on. Is not life greater [in quality] than food, and the body [far above and more excellent] than clothing?
>
> Look at the birds of the air; they neither sow nor reap nor gather into barns, and yet your heavenly Father keeps feeding them. Are you not worth much more than they?
>
> And who of you by worrying and being anxious can add one unit of measure (cubit) to his stature or to the span of his life?
>
> And why should you be anxious about clothes? Consider the lilies of the field and learn thoroughly how they grow; they neither toil nor spin.

> Yet I tell you, even Solomon in all his magnificence (excellence, dignity, and grace) was not arrayed like one of these.
>
> But if God so clothes the grass of the field, which today is alive and green and tomorrow is tossed into the furnace, will He not much more surely clothe you, O you of little faith? Therefore do not worry and be anxious.
>
> —MATTHEW 6:52–31, AMP

Now, you probably know that you shouldn't worry. And maybe you've tried to stop. But here's the reality: God's not merely making a suggestion. He is telling you *don't do it.*

> God knew how to bring those young men out on top, and He knows how to bring *you* out on top, no matter how the devil has tried to turn up the heat on you.

Merriam-Webster's says worry is "to afflict with mental distress or agitation: make anxious."[3] God doesn't want you afflicted with distress or agitation.

He knows that the cares you face living in this world are very real, but He doesn't want you in bondage to them, which is where worrying can take you. The word *worry* reminds me of a dog *worrying* a bone. First he chews and gnaws on it over and over again. Then he takes it outside and buries it in the yard. He puts it out of sight, much like putting questions on a back burner.

But you know what happens with the bone? The dog

goes *back* and digs it up! Then he gnaws on it for another few hours, even though it is dirty and has no more meat on it.

I've done that. I've worried over something, then tried to put it out of my mind, only to go back, dig it up, and start gnawing on it all over again. If you've done it too, just keep smiling as you're reading—no one will know it's you! Be assured, everyone has done it.

But God says *don't*. He says *don't* because He wants you to live a worry-free life, full of peace.

How Do You Stop?

How do you stop worrying? You keep looking into the Word of God, reading it, and believing it. Faith for living worry-free will come by hearing the Word.

> Do not fret or have any anxiety about anything, but in every circumstance and in everything, by prayer and petition (definite requests), with thanksgiving, continue to make your wants known to God. And God's peace [shall be yours, that tranquil state of a soul assured of its salvation through Christ, and so fearing nothing from God and being content with its earthly lot of whatever sort that is, that peace] which transcends all understanding shall garrison and mount guard over your hearts and minds in Christ Jesus.
>
> —PHILIPPIANS 4:6–7, AMP

We like that the part about having God's peace—everyone needs it. But notice there is a condition. No fretting! No anxiety! Who's in charge of not fretting or being anxious? You are. Check out 1 Peter 5:7: "Casting the whole of your care [all your anxieties, all your worries, all your concerns, once and for all] on Him, for He cares for you affectionately and cares about you watchfully" (AMP).

God doesn't want you afflicted
with distress or agitation.

I like to read that verse in the J. B. Phillips translation: "You can throw the whole weight of your anxieties upon him, for you are his *personal concern*" (emphasis added). Think about it—you are God's personal concern!

I like to compare this truth to being the personal concern of the governor or some other important person. Of course, the governor is concerned with the well-being of *all* the people in his state. Everyone is the *public* concern of the governor.

But only the governor's family and those people under his immediate jurisdiction are his *personal* concern. Even though the governor of your state is *your* governor, you probably don't have his personal cell phone number. Or even if you somehow have it, you can't call and get him out of bed in the middle of the night to come help you. Only his wife and children can do that, because he is involved in the everyday workings of their lives. They are his *personal* concern.

That is how it is with God and you—you're His *personal* concern! He is personally involved in every detail of your life. When you call, He drops everything to listen. You'll never get His voice mail or a busy signal. You don't have to talk to one of His aides; you have direct access to Him. He cares!

When we know this truth, we can have more confidence in casting our cares onto God. We know He is paying attention to fixing them. We don't have to keep going back to check on them. He has everything covered. It is like Him saying, "Give me that worry. I'll take care of it."

Some people think it is irresponsible not to worry, suggesting that you are hiding your head in the sand and ignoring a problem if you don't worry about it. But that is not what the Bible means by casting your cares on God. To cast your cares on Him is to turn them over and *believe* Him! It is still a faith exercise.

I'll give you an example of how some people feel about casting their cares on God. When I fly, I don't like to schlep all my luggage around with me. I like to check it. So I go to the counter, and I *cast the care* of my luggage over to the airlines.

However, if you've flown more than a few times, you know that there's always a chance that my luggage might not arrive at my destination at the same time as I do. In other words, when I cast the care of my luggage onto the airlines, I'm not always sure it will arrive safe and sound. Why? Because I don't believe that the airlines *care* about my luggage the way I do.

But if I *knew they cared*, I wouldn't worry so much. Of course, even airline employees who care are imperfect and there could still be a mistake. With a perfect God I have full assurance that not only does He care but He can also deliver no matter what happens.

When you bathe your spirit in God's Word and come

to a working knowledge of His care and personal concern for you, you'll think more about what God says than what the worry says. You'll be able to safely cast your worries onto Him, knowing He will take care of them.

Cast Your Cares on God Today

The only way you're going to come out on top in life is if you cast your cares on God and refuse to worry. Don't wait another minute. Do it today. Be very purposeful. Begin by writing down your worries. This will help you in several ways.

> Think about it—you are
> God's personal concern!

First, it will help you see that there are not as many concerns as you thought there were. When worries are left unhindered to roam around in your mind, they grow. And pretty soon you start to feel as if everything is wrong. But that is not true. Writing down your concerns puts a limit on them.

Second, find what the Bible says about each of these worries. Line up God's Word next to your cares, and let it take dominion.

Third, pray the following words and believe them:

Father God, in Jesus's name, I love You, and I'm going to obey Your Word. I'm casting my cares onto You. I'm not going to carry them anymore. I'm going to trust You. I refuse to worry anymore! I will keep my eyes on Your Word and believe You. I'll stay in faith. My problems aren't stuck to me anymore. They're stuck to You! I know You care for me. I know You're taking care of my problems, so I don't have to worry about them. I listen to Your voice, I'll do what You say to do, and from now on I'll live a life that's free of care! Amen.

Now Engage

God thinks you are coming out on top. Build faith that He will always cause you to triumph by meditating on and declaring these truths from God's Word.

Front-Burner Truth: "I know that I'm still coming out on top."

> And we know that all things work together for good to those who love God, to those who are the called according to His purpose.
>
> —ROMANS 8:28

God is working things out for me. He always causes me to triumph (2 Cor. 2:14). If anyone is going to come out on top in my current situation, it's going to be me! God knows how to take horrible things that have happened to me and work them together for my good. If it's not good yet, then my story just isn't over! I know and believe that God will bring me out of all my troubles.

> The LORD was with Joseph, and he was a successful man; and he was in the house of his master the Egyptian.
>
> —GENESIS 39:2

If God was with Joseph as a slave and a prisoner, He's with me too, no matter what. So like Joseph, I'm going to work hard, use my God-given skills, keep a good attitude, and expect the supernatural. I will rise up in the midst of my circumstances and remember the dream in my heart. I can excel in the midst of trouble!

> Rejoice in the Lord always. Again I will say, rejoice!
> —Philippians 4:4

> The only way you're going to come out on top in life is if you cast your cares on God and refuse to worry.

If Paul could rejoice in prison, then I can constantly rejoice in the middle of what's going on with me. I will release God's power through praise, which can also help everyone around me get free too.

> Our God whom we serve is able to deliver us from the burning fiery furnace, and He will deliver us from your hand, O king.
> —Daniel 3:17

Shadrach, Meshach, and Abednego didn't bow under pressure; they had faith in God. I won't bow to the devil's pressure either, because I have faith in God too. When the heat is turned up, my heavenly Father knows how to bring me out on top. I will listen to His voice, follow His lead, and end up walking away not even smelling like smoke. And people will be telling my testimony for a long time too, all to God's glory!

Casting the whole of your care [all your anxieties, all your worries, all your concerns, once and for all] on Him, for He cares for you affectionately and cares about you watchfully.

—1 PETER 5:7, AMP

God hears me, so I refuse to worry. I am His personal concern—He cares for me completely. When I call, He drops everything to listen to me. I'll never get His voice mail or a busy signal. I have complete confidence in casting my cares onto Him. I know He's paying attention to fixing my problems. I believe Him!

Chapter Eleven

IN THE END YOU WIN!

HERE IS ANOTHER front-burner truth to focus on, something you know to be true: when it is all said and done, you win! It is *crucial* to know where you're ultimately going to end up and to keep your eyes on the prize. After you've lived your life to the fullest, you are headed for heaven.

Second Corinthians 5:8 says, "We are confident, yes, well pleased rather to be absent from the body and to be present with the Lord." As a Christian, when you leave your earthly body behind, you can be confident of going to heaven and being present with God for all eternity! The Bible says that now, here on earth, you see spiritual things dimly, with only partial understanding, but in heaven, you'll see and understand things; you'll see Jesus face to face.

The Message says it this way, "We don't yet see things clearly. We're squinting in a fog, peering through a mist. But it won't be long before the weather clears and the sun shines bright! We'll see it all then, see it all as clearly as God sees us, knowing him directly just as he knows us!" (1 Cor. 13:12).

Right now you have questions. I know some people who say, "When I get to heaven, I'm going to ask God about this!" But I think many of those questions will fall away once you get to heaven. For starters you'll automatically understand things you don't understand now. And for another thing heaven is going to be so wonderful that your questions—things you thought were so important here on earth—just won't be that important anymore. You simply won't care as you enjoy an atmosphere of complete love, health, and peace.

> After you've lived your life to the fullest, you are headed for heaven.

Heaven Will Be Your Eternal Home

What a hope we have! You have much to look forward to because like the apostle Paul, you know where you're going. Paul said, "To live is Christ, to die is *gain*" (Phil. 1:21, emphasis added). He knew that to be with Christ in heaven is *far better* than life here on earth (v. 23).

Whenever someone says to me, "I'm sorry you lost your husband," I always answer, "Oh, I didn't lose him. I know *right* when he is!" He is in a place that is far better. He has *gained!* There is such a peace of mind in knowing that.

If you've had a loved one die, you don't have to worry that you'll never see him again. If he or she received Jesus, you'll spend eternity together. Right now that person is safely tucked away in heaven, seeing Jesus face-to-face, walking on streets of gold, and having a great time.

When you get there, your loved one won't say, "What took you so long?" Why? Because there is no time in heaven, at least not like time is measured here on earth. It is eternity. We don't really know what it will be like, but I like to think that your loved one will just say, "Oh good, you're here. Let's go!" And then he or she will show you around the place.

When you look at your life in the frame of eternity, you see that you're here on earth for a very short time. In that light it is so important to make every moment count. It is also crucial to share Jesus with your friends and loved ones to make sure they go to heaven for eternity as well. If you've had a loved one die and you aren't sure the person was saved, take comfort in the fact that God is good. I believe He gives each person many chances to receive Him, right up to the very end. We don't know what your loved one might have heard in his lifetime, what decisions he may have made, or what happened to him right before he left this earth. My spiritual father used to say, "We're going to be surprised by who we find in heaven." I believe that.

I like to think about heaven, perhaps because my husband, Brent, is already there. I don't think about it so much that I'm not living my life to the fullest. I'm not looking to escape or go there a moment before I've finished my course, but I get excited thinking about the place. It is where you and I are headed, and it is going to be so great.

Because of the Fall, when sin entered the world, you live on an earth that has a curse. You were born here, and you simply have no idea what it is like to live free from it. Yes, *you* have been redeemed from the curse

(Gal. 3:13), but the earth has not. Even though you have authority now, in Christ, to live above the curse, you're still surrounded by sin, sickness, fear, oppression, and more. This feels normal because it's all you've ever known.

Thankfully, in our eternal home of heaven, there is no curse—no fear or sickness or death or sadness. Only light, life, and love permeate the entire atmosphere of heaven. I think that when you get there, no matter how much you've heard about the place and how great you've expected it to be, you will walk around for a millennium or so with your mouth hanging open because it is so wonderful! Right now, you can't even comprehend it.

No matter how good you think heaven is, it is better. And you are a citizen there! Philippians 3:20–21 says, "Our citizenship is in heaven, and from it we await a Savior, the Lord Jesus Christ, who will transform our lowly body to be like his glorious body, by the power that enables him even to subject all things to himself" (ESV).

> In our eternal home of heaven, there is no curse—no fear or sickness or death or sadness.

As soon as you became born again, you became a brand-new creature (2 Cor. 5:17) and subsequently a foreigner on this earth. When you chose Jesus—the way to heaven (John 14:6)—you became a citizen of heaven. And when you get there, you'll have a new and glorious body just as He does (1 Cor. 15:42–53).

Jesus promised that He would prepare a place for you

there in heaven (John 14:2). When you arrive, you'll see Him not in a picture, not from far away, but face-to-face. You'll walk with Him on streets that are pure gold (Rev. 21:21)—not just paved with gold but made of gold!

Revelation 21 describes heaven in great detail. It says, "He will wipe away every tear from their eyes, and death shall be no more, neither shall there be mourning, nor crying, nor pain anymore, for the former things have passed away" (Rev. 21:4, ESV). I encourage you to read the entire chapter for yourself.

Heaven is such good news! You can rejoice right now because you're headed somewhere great. Yes, hard things may have happened to you on this earth, and you may have questions, but keep everything in perspective. Life is just a blip on the screen of eternity. When Jesus is your Savior, in the end you win.

Run Your Race

The Bible says, "Let us lay aside every weight, and the sin which so easily ensnares us, and let us run with endurance the race that is set before us" (Heb. 12:1). First Corinthians 9:24–25 says, "Do you not know that those who run in a race all run, but one receives the prize? Run in such a way that you may obtain it. And everyone who competes for the prize is temperate in all things. Now they do it to obtain a perishable crown, but we for an imperishable crown."

This verse describes how to run and why to run. Let's face it, the whole reason for running in a race is to win! So no matter what has happened and what questions you have simmering on a back burner, it is important to keep focusing on this race that is your life.

While on earth keep running strong, even if you have questions. The whole reason you're still here on earth is to be a blessing. Think about it: when you got saved, you became a citizen of heaven. Why didn't you just move to your new home after you accepted Christ? Because God needs you here on earth. He needs you to fulfill His plan and to bring others with you when you come. So keep your eyes on what is important.

> No matter what has happened....
> it is important to keep focusing
> on this race that is your life.

Remember that your life on earth has a beginning and an end. While here it is essential that you focus on the finish line and the imperishable crown that awaits you on the other side. Finish strong!

The apostle Paul had a strong finish to his race. And horrible things happened to him along the way. But he didn't quit. He didn't let his questions keep him out of the race. His life is a great example.

When Paul was headed for Jerusalem (where he knew he was going to end up in prison), Paul said, "But none of these things move me; nor do I count my life dear to myself, so that I may *finish my race* with joy, and the ministry which I received from the Lord Jesus, to testify to the gospel of the grace of God" (Acts 20:24, emphasis added).

At the end of Paul's life he told Timothy, "I have fought the good fight, I have finished the race, I have kept the faith" (2 Tim. 4:7). When it is time for me to go heaven,

I want to be able to say I finished the race. I didn't quit. I kept the faith. I want to be able to see that my life was a blessing and a help to others, and know that I'm finally headed for my reward.

Anybody can start a race. It is how you finish that counts. Even when life throws you some tough blows, it is not over until it's over. Your focus determines how you finish. I remember watching a track and field event during which two runners were neck and neck toward the end. Just as they approached the finish line, the runner who was barely in the lead turned his head to glance at the other runner. I suppose he wanted to see how close his competitor was. In that millisecond he slowed his stride and lost the race. He hadn't realized the other runner was only inches behind him. When he took his focus off the finish line to look back, he lost the edge.

There is something to learn from that runner. First, *run your own race.* Don't worry about what anyone else is doing. The race the other runner is running isn't your race. He isn't called to do what you're called to do, and vice versa. If you get distracted by someone else's race, you'll lose your focus and it may cost you, just as it cost that runner.

The second point to learn is that *you can't take your eyes off of the finish line.* There are many things—good and bad—that will come along and compete for your attention. Stay focused.

Don't Get Distracted

I once heard a story that illustrates the concept of getting distracted and taking your eyes off what is really important. The story is about a man who ordered a hamburger at a drive-up window of a fast-food restaurant. He received his food and drove away, unwrapping the burger and beginning to eat as he pulled his vehicle onto the street.

Anybody can start a race. It is
how you finish that counts

He hadn't gone far when he took a big bite and a pickle squirted out of the burger. It plopped onto the leg of his pants. Don't you hate it when that happens?

With one hand he gripped the steering wheel. With the other hand he grabbed a napkin and attempted to remove the pickle before any juice soaked into his pants. He just about had the pickle when he glanced up at the street. Suddenly his heart was in his throat. While his attention had been diverted to the pickle, his car had veered into oncoming traffic, and a semitruck was bearing down on him!

With his adrenaline pumping like crazy, he grabbed the steering wheel with both hands and jerked his car back into his own lane, just milliseconds before impact. The near-miss shook him so much that he had to pull over, and that is when he heard the Lord speak to his heart, "Son, don't get distracted. Keep looking *forward*, and don't focus on the pickle on your pants."

The man knew instantly that God was telling him something important about life. There will always be "pickles," little things that happen every day that clamor to grab your focus and distract you from what really matters.

Maybe the distraction is the dog tracking dirt into the house, your coworker annoying you, or a traffic jam making you late for an appointment. Maybe it is something bigger such as disease, economic troubles, or a bad report. It happens to my students. They leave their homes and forsake all to come to school, but then they get distracted by roommates, jobs, bills, or irritating people.

You *do* have to deal with details in life, but guard against letting them fill your view. Instead of getting distracted, be like Jesus, who is "the author and finisher of our faith, who for the joy that was set before Him endured the cross, despised the shame and sat down at the right hand of the throne of God" (Heb. 12:2).

Notice that Jesus endured the suffering of the cross by keeping His eyes on "the joy set before Him." There is joy set before you—your calling and purpose here on earth, and eventually your place in heaven. Focus on those things! Don't let the pickles on your pants take all your attention. As author Richard Carlson says, "Don't sweat the small stuff."[1]

When I find myself in a pickle-on-my-pants moment, I ask myself: "Will this matter in ten years? Ten months? Ten days? Ten hours?" If the answer is no to any question but the first one, it is not worth much attention.

Yes, you have to take care of things as they come up, but at the same time don't take your eyes off the windshield. Keep your focus on what really matters.

Now Engage

In the end you win! Meditating on and declaring these truths will help you keep your eyes on the prize—you are headed for heaven!

Front-Burner Truth: "I know that in the end I win."

> We are confident, yes, well pleased rather to be absent from the body and to be present with the Lord.
>
> —2 CORINTHIANS 5:8

When I leave my earthly body behind, I am confident that I'm going to heaven. I win! I will be present with God forever! In the frame of eternity I'm here on earth for a very short time, so I'll make every moment count. I'll also share Jesus with my friends and loved ones to make sure they go to heaven for eternity as well. Meanwhile I'll keep my eyes on the prize and live life to the fullest.

> To live is Christ, and to die is *gain.*
>
> —PHILIPPIANS 1:21,
> EMPHASIS ADDED

I have so much to look forward to—I know where I'm going! In my eternal home of heaven there's no curse—no fear or sickness or death or sadness or even dirt. Only light and life and love permeate the entire atmosphere. What a hope we have.

> Let us lay aside every weight, and the sin which so easily ensnares us, and let us run with endurance the race that is set before us.
>
> —HEBREWS 12:1

No matter what has happened and what questions I have simmering on the back burner, I'll lay aside life's weights and run my race with endurance. I'll remember that it has a beginning and an end. I'll run my own race and not worry about anyone else's. I'll keep my eyes on the finish line and the reward that awaits me on the other side.

> Looking unto Jesus, the author and finisher of our faith, who for the joy that was set before Him endured the cross, despising the shame, and has sat down at the right hand of the throne of God.
> —HEBREWS 12:2

Just as Jesus did, I'll keep my eyes on the joy set before me. I won't get distracted but will concentrate on the things that really matter in life. I won't sweat the small stuff! I'll take care of things as they come up, but I won't take my eyes off the windshield.

> The path of the righteous is like the light of dawn, that shines brighter and brighter until the full day.
> —PROVERBS 4:18, NAS

I believe my life is getting better and better, not dimmer and dimmer! God thinks my best days are ahead of me. I'm not declining; I'm getting brighter and brighter. I'm gaining more wisdom, more knowledge, more ability to help people, and more possibility to bless others. I'm embracing the next season of my life and believing that the best is yet to come. God has great things in store for me.

Conclusion

FOCUS FORWARD

W HEN YOU STARTED reading this book, I know you had questions. I hope that now you've gone through these pages, your questions are simmering away on the back burner of your life. And I hope you have some fresh hope and energy to continue "cooking" with God on your front burners!

I've enjoyed spending this time with you. Know that I am praying for you! Meanwhile, I encourage you to return often to the powerful "Now Engage" sections at the end of each chapter and continue to speak God's Word over your life and your circumstances. He is faithful to perform it in your life and to keep moving you forward *through* the valley of shadow until the hurt of the past is only a memory. If you'll do that, and follow the principles we've talked about, you'll get there. I'm believing with you!

The Best Is Yet to Come

Not long after my husband died, I read Ecclesiastes 7:8, which says, "The end of something is better than its beginning" (GNT).

I took this verse to heart. My life with Brent had been great, and I missed him a lot, but I decided to believe that life could get better. That sounds like what God would want, don't you think? He knows how to make your ending even better than your beginning.

Proverbs 4:18 says, "The path of the righteous is like the light of dawn, that shines brighter and brighter until the full day" (NAS). According to this verse the path of your life is getting brighter and brighter, not dimmer and dimmer.

God thinks your greatest days are ahead of you. You're not declining, you're increasing. As you grow older, you have more wisdom, knowledge, ability to help people and possibility to bless others. You cannot begin to imagine all the good things God has planned for you.

Be inspired by a quote from Helen Keller: "Life is either a great adventure or nothing."[1] Your life with God can be a great adventure.

Be encouraged. Your questions are secure on the back burner, and you are moving forward. I'm proud of you! As you embrace the next season of your life with expectation and faith, know that with Jesus, the best truly *is* yet to come.

Prayer of Salvation

MAYBE YOU'RE READING this book because you have questions, but you've never met the God you're seeking answers from. Maybe you've never asked Him into your life. I want to invite you into a relationship with Him. He holds all the answers, He knows you inside and out, and He loves you! He knows what your heart desires.

There was a point in my life when I had to be introduced to Him, just like anyone who is a Christian. Now I can honestly say, if it wasn't for Him in my life, I wouldn't be where I am today. We are all born into sin (Rom. 3:23). Sin separates you from God. Two thousand years ago God sent His only Son, Jesus, to the earth as a man, and He died on the cross to bear the consequences of our sin so that we could be restored to a perfect relationship (right standing) with God (1 Pet. 2:24). He became sin so that we could become righteousness (2 Cor. 5:21). He traded places with us.

God loves you, not because you've done everything right or because you're good, but because *He* is good. He loved you so much that He sent Jesus to pay a price you could never pay (John 3:16). He wants to have a personal, one-on-one, day-to-day relationship with you. You are the apple of His eye (Ps. 17:8).

It is God's will for you to be saved. If you've never received Jesus as your Savior, then you've never received the benefits of what He did for you on the cross, and you're still in a sinful state.

You can receive Him today. It is not hard. The Bible says:

> If you confess with your mouth the Lord Jesus and believe in your heart that God has raised Him from the dead, you will be saved. For with the heart one believes unto righteousness, and with the mouth confession is made unto salvation. For the Scripture says, "Whoever believes on Him will not be put to shame." For there is no distinction between Jew and Greek, for the same Lord over all is rich to all who call upon Him. For "whoever calls on the name of the LORD shall be saved."
>
> —ROMANS 10:9–13

All of God's blessings and the benefits of salvation can be yours if you receive Him into your heart. You can do this by praying this prayer:

> *Dear God, I come to You admitting that I am a sinner. I believe that Your Son, Jesus, died on the cross to take away my sins. I also believe He rose from the dead so I could be justified and made righteous through faith in Him. I call upon the name of Jesus Christ to be the Savior and Lord of my life. Jesus, thank You for washing away my sin. I choose to follow You, and I ask that You fill me with the power of the Holy Spirit. I declare right now that I am a born-again child of God. I am free from sin, and I am the righteousness of God in Christ. I am saved, in Jesus's name. Amen.*

Congratulations, and welcome to the family of God! If you prayed that prayer for the first time, I'd like to hear from you so that I can send you a special gift. Please contact me through the website listed on the About the Author page. I also encourage you to get into a good, Word-believing church so you can learn and grow.

Notes

Chapter One
Is It OK to Question God?

1. Wikiquote.org, "Sleepless in Seattle," http://en.wikiquote
.org/wiki/Sleepless_in_Seattle (accessed March 5, 2013).
2. Earl Nightingale, *Lead the Field: Lesson 1: The Magic
Word and Acres of Diamonds* (n.p.: BN Publishing, 2006).
3. The author of this story is unknown. For many years it
has been retold in various forms by various people, including a
revised retelling by Joel Osteen in his book *Every Day a Friday*
(New York: FaithWords, 2011).

Chapter 2
He'll Never Let You God

1. *Merriam-Webster's Collegiate Dictionary*, 11th edition
(Springfield, MA: Merriam-Webster, Inc., 2003), s.v. "ravish."

Chapter 5
One Thing *Never* Changes

1. W. E. Vine, *Vine's Expository Dictionary of New Testament Words*, "Doubt (Be In, Make To), Doubtful, Doubting,"
Blue Letter Bible, http://www.blueletterbible.org/Search/
Dictionary/viewTopic.cfm?type=getTopic&Topic=Doubt+(Be+In
%2C+Make+To)%2C+Doubtful%2C+Doubting (accessed March
7, 2013).

Chapter 6
There's a Blueprint for Your Life

1. Brainy Quote, "Friedrich Nietzsche quotes," http://
www.brainyquote.com/quotes/quotes/f/friedrichn101616.html
(accessed March 7, 2013).

Chapter 7
God Is Still in the Multiplication Business

1. *Merriam-Webster's Collegiate Dictionary*, s.v. "hope."

Chapter 8
You Haven't Lost Your Place

1. John C. Maxwell, "The Cost Question," http://www
.johnmaxwell.com/uploads/general/The_Cost_Question.pdf
(accessed March 11, 2013).
2. "Constantly Abiding" by Anne May Sebring Murphy.
Public domain.

Chapter 9
You Are Loved

1. *Merriam-Webster's Collegiate Dictionary*, s.v. "tabernacle."

Chapter 10
God Still Thinks You're Coming Out on Top

1. ThinkExist.com, "Leo F. Buscaglia Quotes," http://
thinkexist.com/quotation/worry_never_robs_tomorrow_of_its_
sorrow-it_only/213606.html (accessed March 12, 2013).
2. Corrie ten Boom, "Corrie ten Boom Quotes," http://www
.goodreads.com/author/quotes/102203.Corrie_ten_Boom
(accessed March 12, 2013)
3. *Merriam-Webster's Collegiate Dictionary*, s.v. "worry."

Chapter 11
In the End You Win!

1. Richard Carlson, *Don't Sweat the Small Stuff—and It's
all Small Stuff* (New York, NY: Hyperion, 1997).

Conclusion
Focus Forward

1. ThinkExist.com, "Helen Keller Quotes," http://thinkexist
.com/quotation/life_is_either_a_great_adventure_or_nothing/
208353.html (accessed February 1, 2013).

About the Author

KAREN JENSEN HAS been in ministry for almost thirty years and a writer for almost forty. She and her husband, Brent, traveled as itinerant ministers and also pioneered two churches in the Northwest.

In 1997, upon Brent's unexpected death, she became senior pastor of their church in Boise, Idaho. She raised their sons, Josh and Ryan, through their teenage years into young men on fire for God.

Now an instructor at Rhema Bible Training College in Broken Arrow, Oklahoma, since 2005, Karen also travels across the United States and overseas, sharing what she has learned about the faithfulness of God through good times and bad.

Her teachings and writings have influenced the lives of hundreds of thousands of people all over the world. Her humor, her never-give-up attitude, her love for God, and her strong stand on His Word will bless and inspire you.

Karen Jensen
MINISTRIES

Visit Karen at her website www.karenjensen.org, where you can

- Contact her personally—she'd love to hear from you
- Book her for speaking engagements
- Shop for CDs, DVDs, devotionals, etc.
- Watch videos of Karen
- Read her blogs "Parenting With Faith" and "This Is the Life"
- Be encouraged by her archived teachings
- Follow her itinerary
- *And more...*

Check out Rhema Bible Training College where Karen teaches at www.rbtc.org.

LET KAREN JENSEN ENCOURAGE YOU WITH GOD'S WORD

2-CD series. If you're like most of us, you've had painful things happen to you. But God doesn't want you to stay hurt. Learn how to cut the chains of hurt and live a life of forgiveness.

3-CD series. You've never been loved like this before! Learn more about how *you* are the focus of God's everlasting love, and believing that love will change in every way.

CD or DVD. These powerful and practical Bible-based lessons have helped families around the world, and can equip and encourage any parent, no matter the age of their child.

- 16 half-hour lessons
- Great for personal use or group study (cell groups, church classes, special meetings, community outreach)
- Workbooks and group leader workbook available
- 31-day devotional for parents

ORDER THESE AND OTHER PRODUCTS FROM
WWW.KARENJENSEN.ORG

World Vision®

Building a better world for children

Who we are:

World Vision is a Christian humanitarian organization dedicated to working with children, families, and their communities worldwide to reach their full potential by tackling the causes of poverty and injustice. Working in nearly 100 countries around the world, World Vision serves all people, regardless of religion, race, ethnicity, or gender.

SPONSORING A CHILD
is the most powerful way *you* can fight poverty

Visit www.WorldVision.org to sponsor a child today.